(5.)

Oh, give me a stream
pool Brights and Deep, in
Those hills where I wonder
where Trout lie asleep, and
Willows that weep, hiding in
a moss covered stone, &

(6.)

I never wood change my H
on The Range, for a Throne
The gold of a king, The Ca~
I see is a palace To me, o
~~Home my sweet home on~~
Range.

End

11/28/44

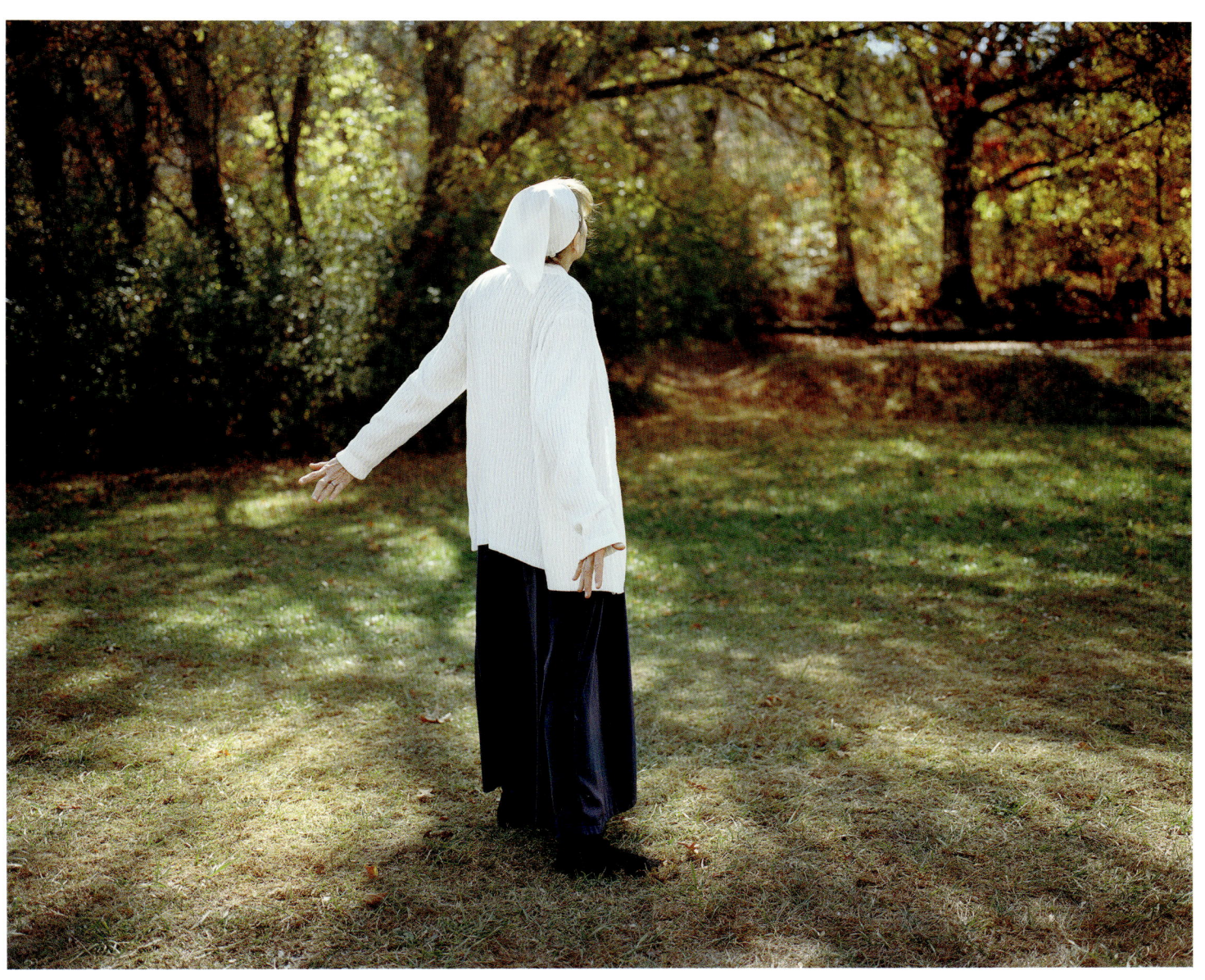

Cofounders: Taj Forer and Michael Itkoff
Creative Director: Ursula Damm
Co-Editors: Rachel Boillot and Sasha Wolf
Copy Editors: Nancy Hubbard, Barbara Richard

ISBN 978-1-942084-67-9

Printed by Artron, China

Daylight Books
E-mail: info@daylightbooks.org
Web: www.daylightbooks.org

MOON SHINE

Rachel Boillot

Daylight

In memory of:

Tom McCarroll,
With whom I collected time

The indomitable spirit of Curtis Byrge

And most of all, for my Evie —
Call yourself what you want to
I will always love you.

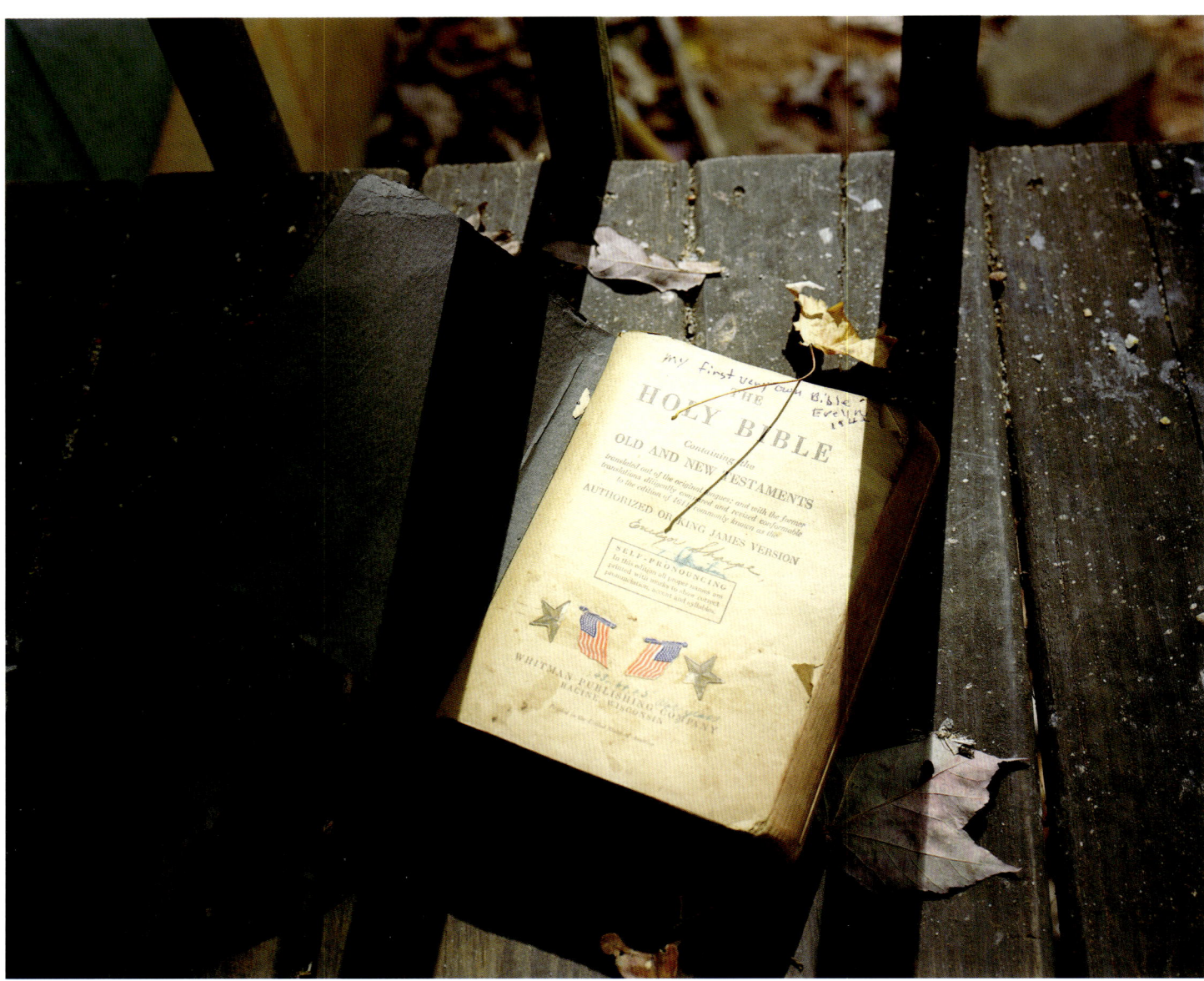

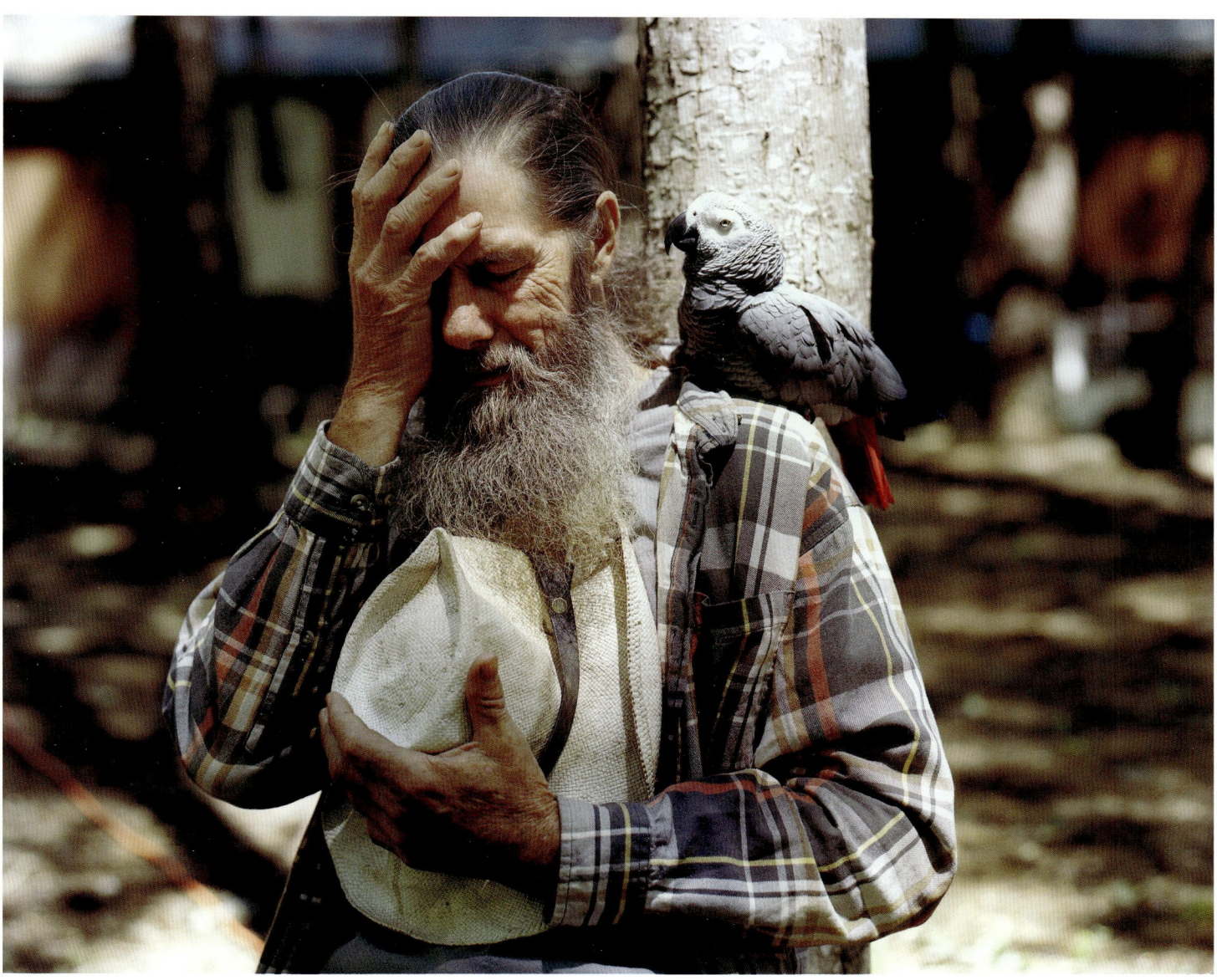

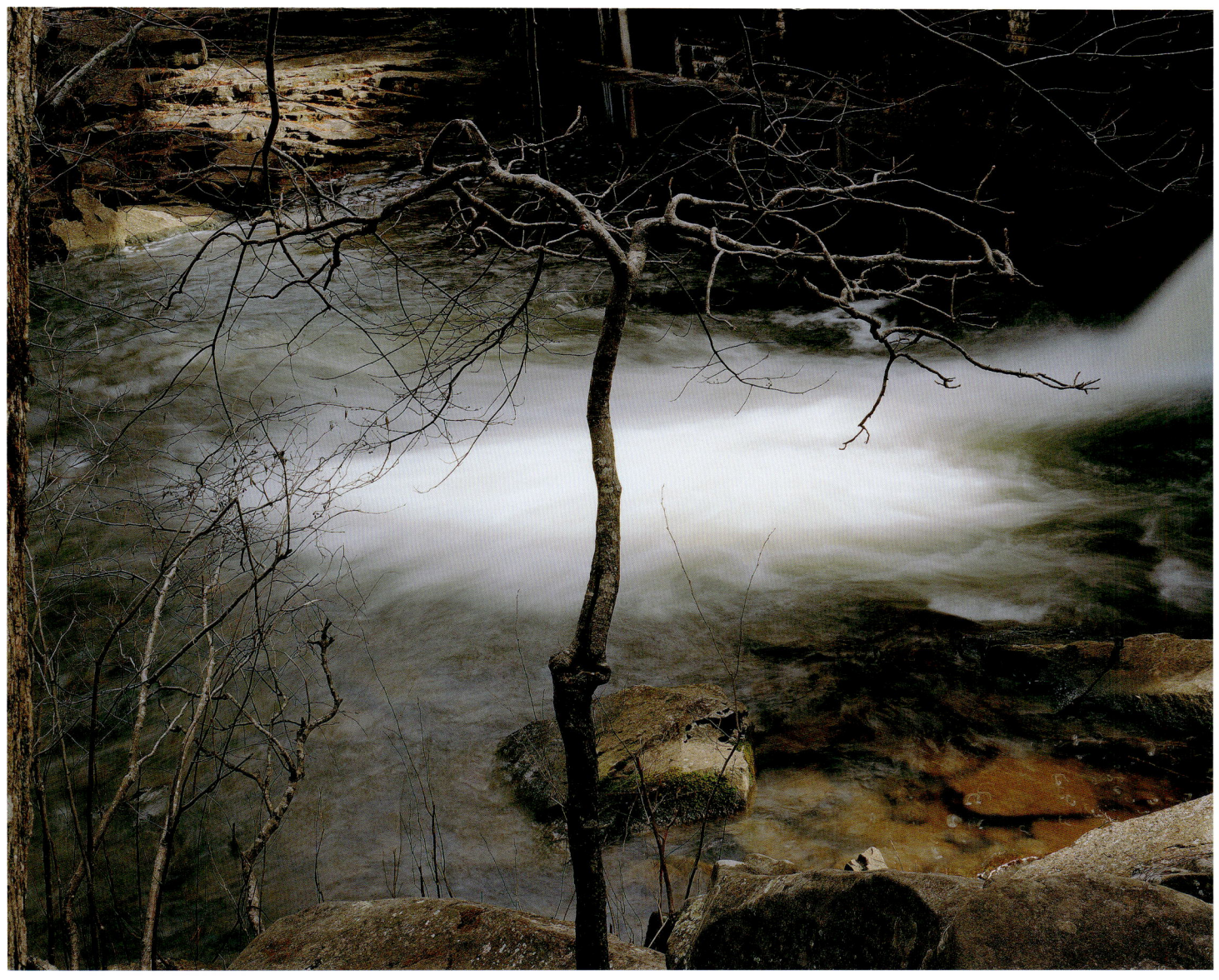

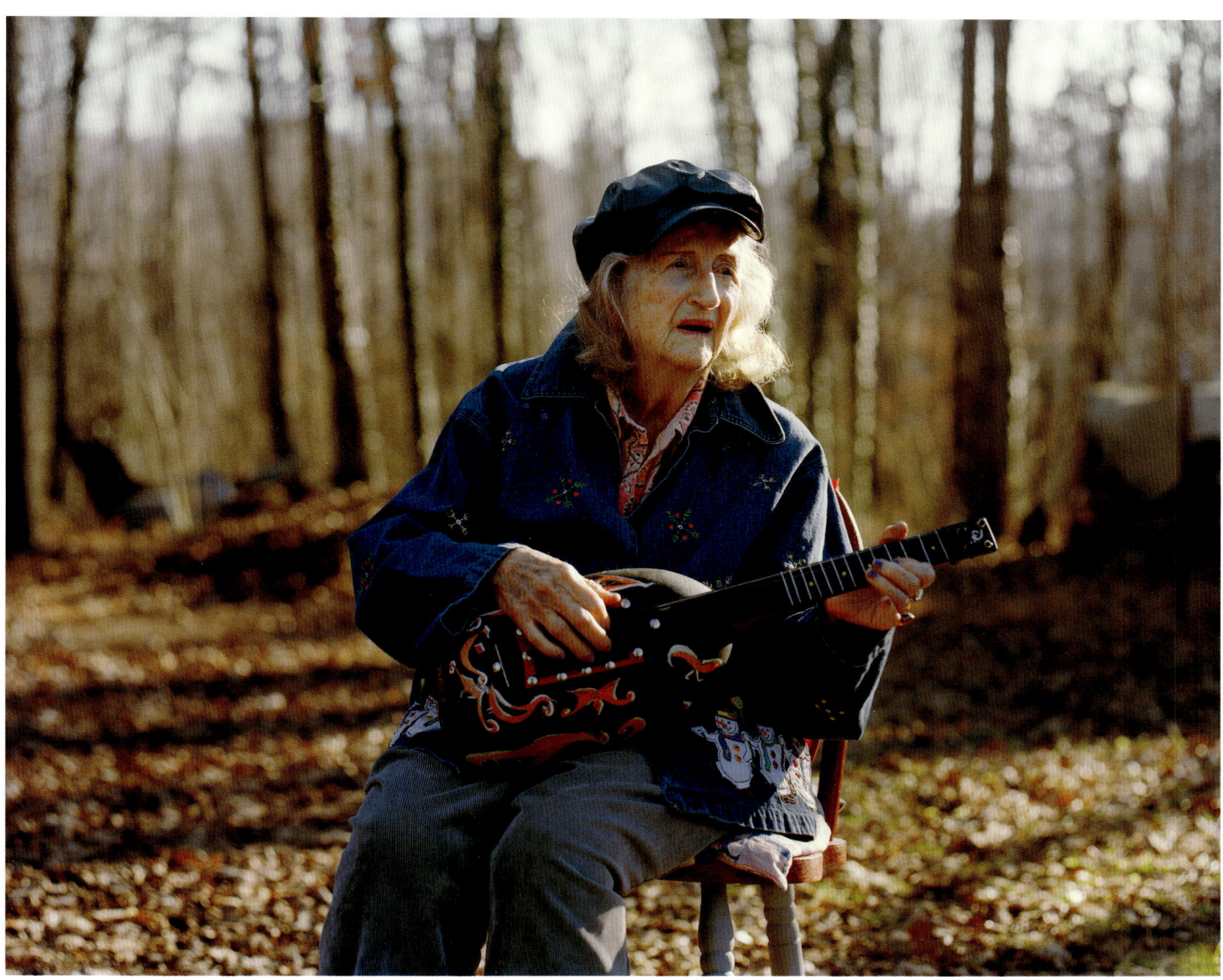

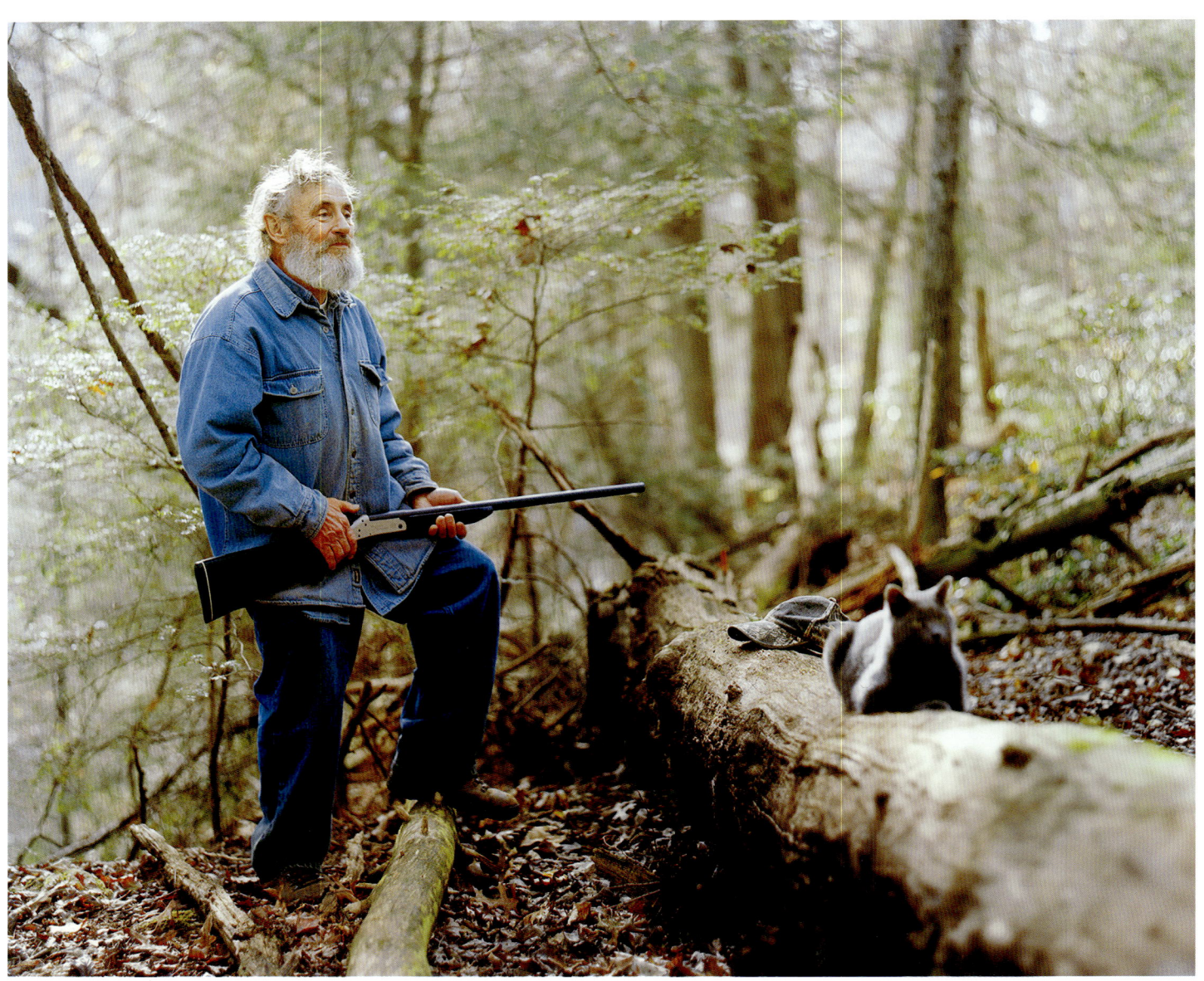

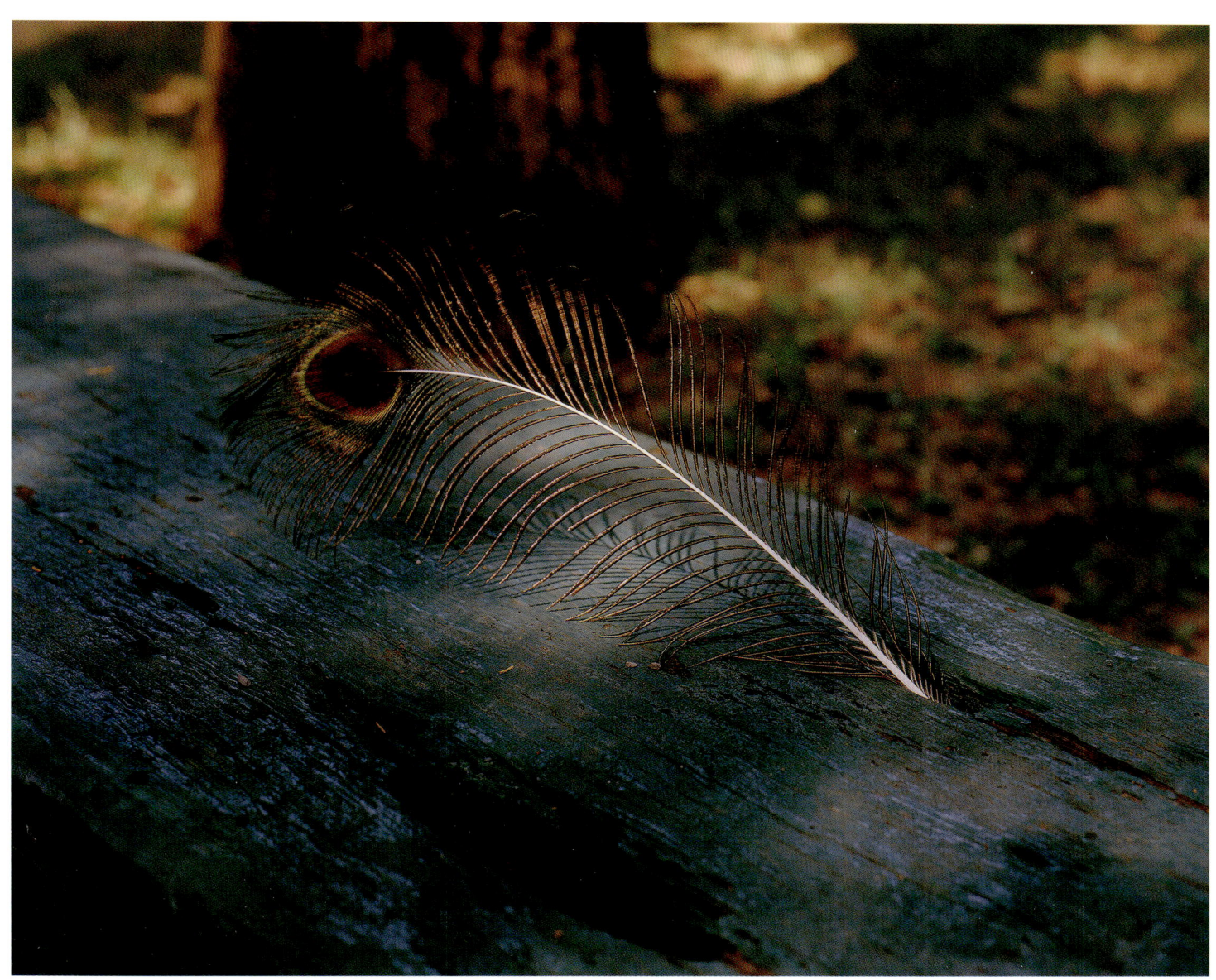

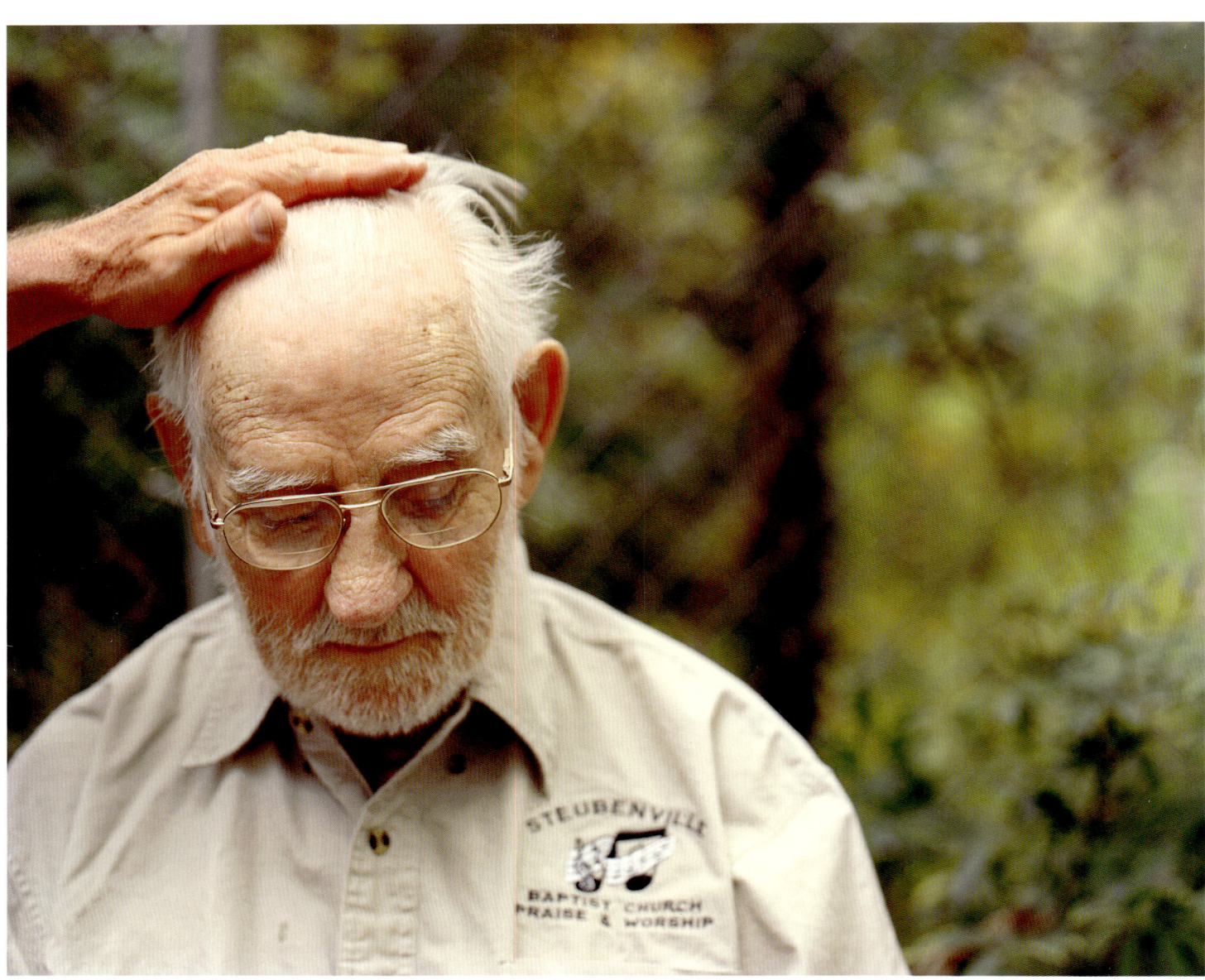

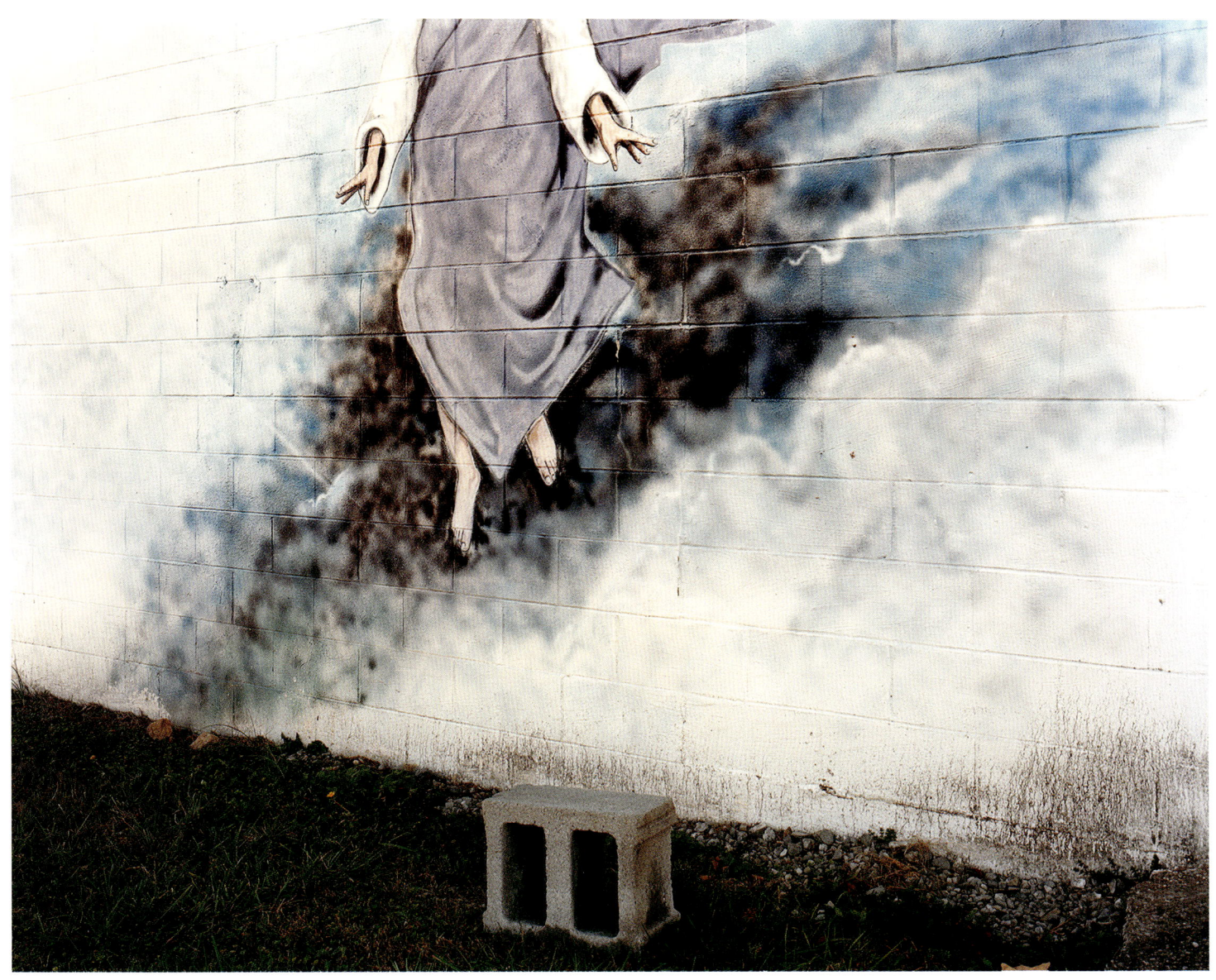

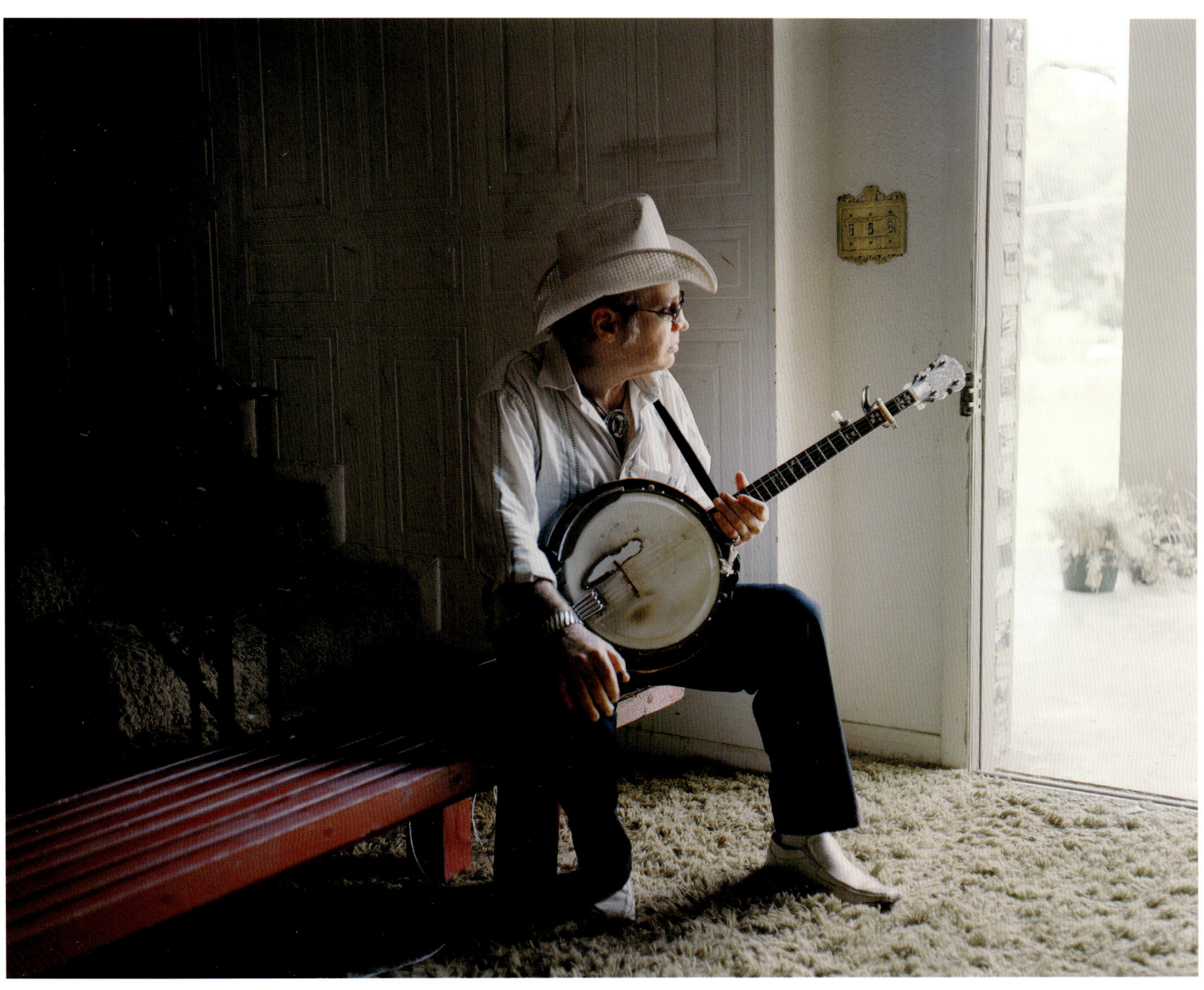

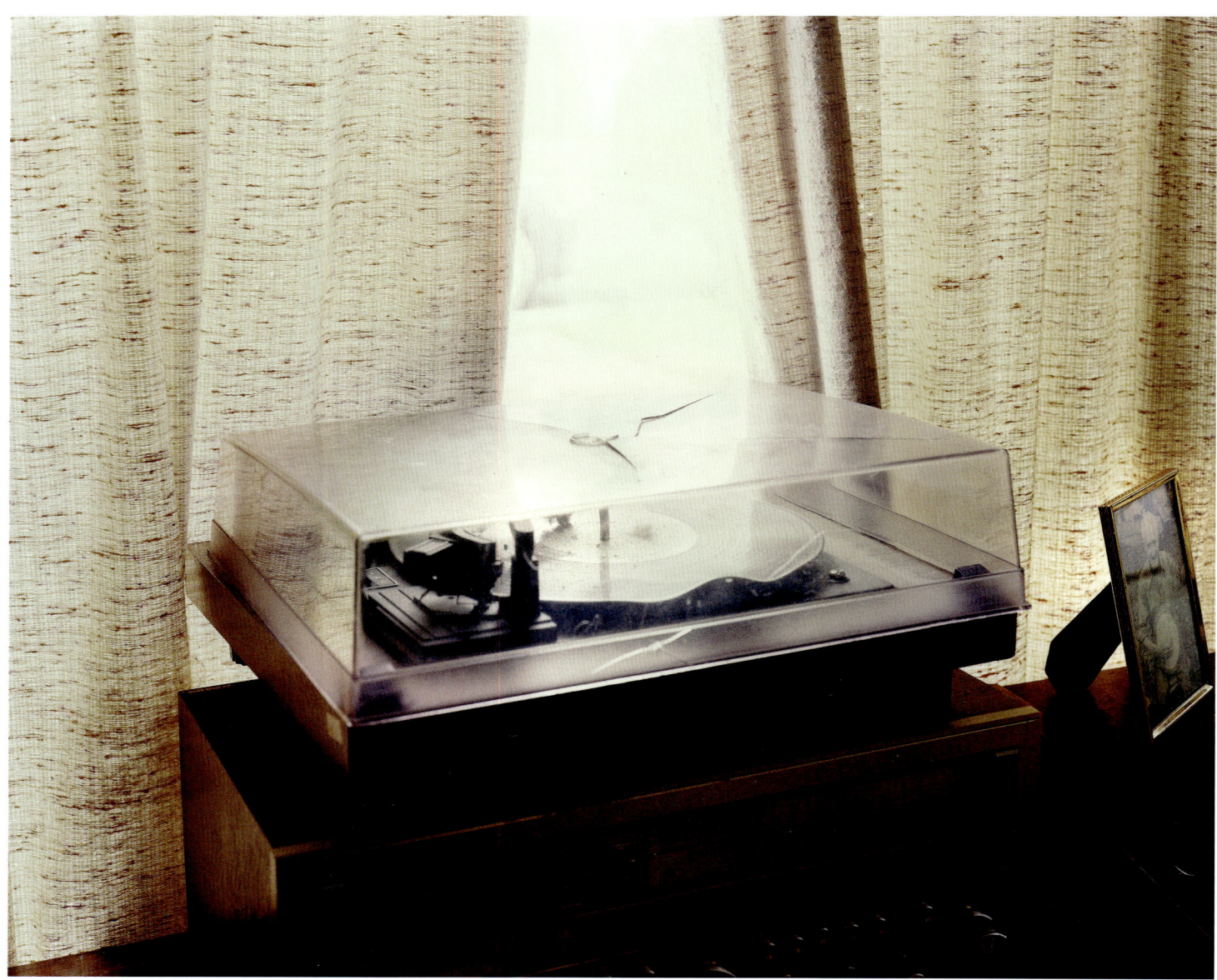

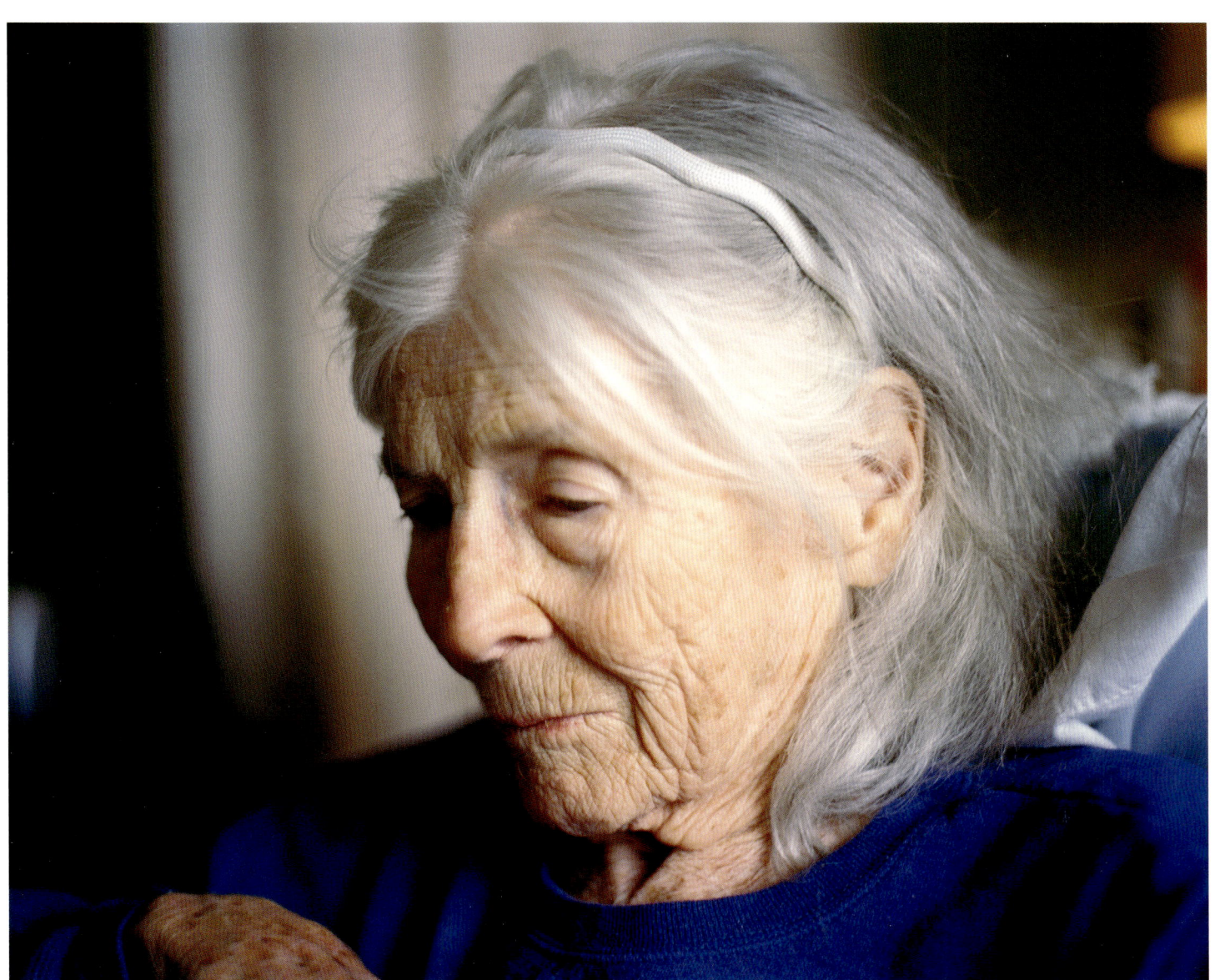

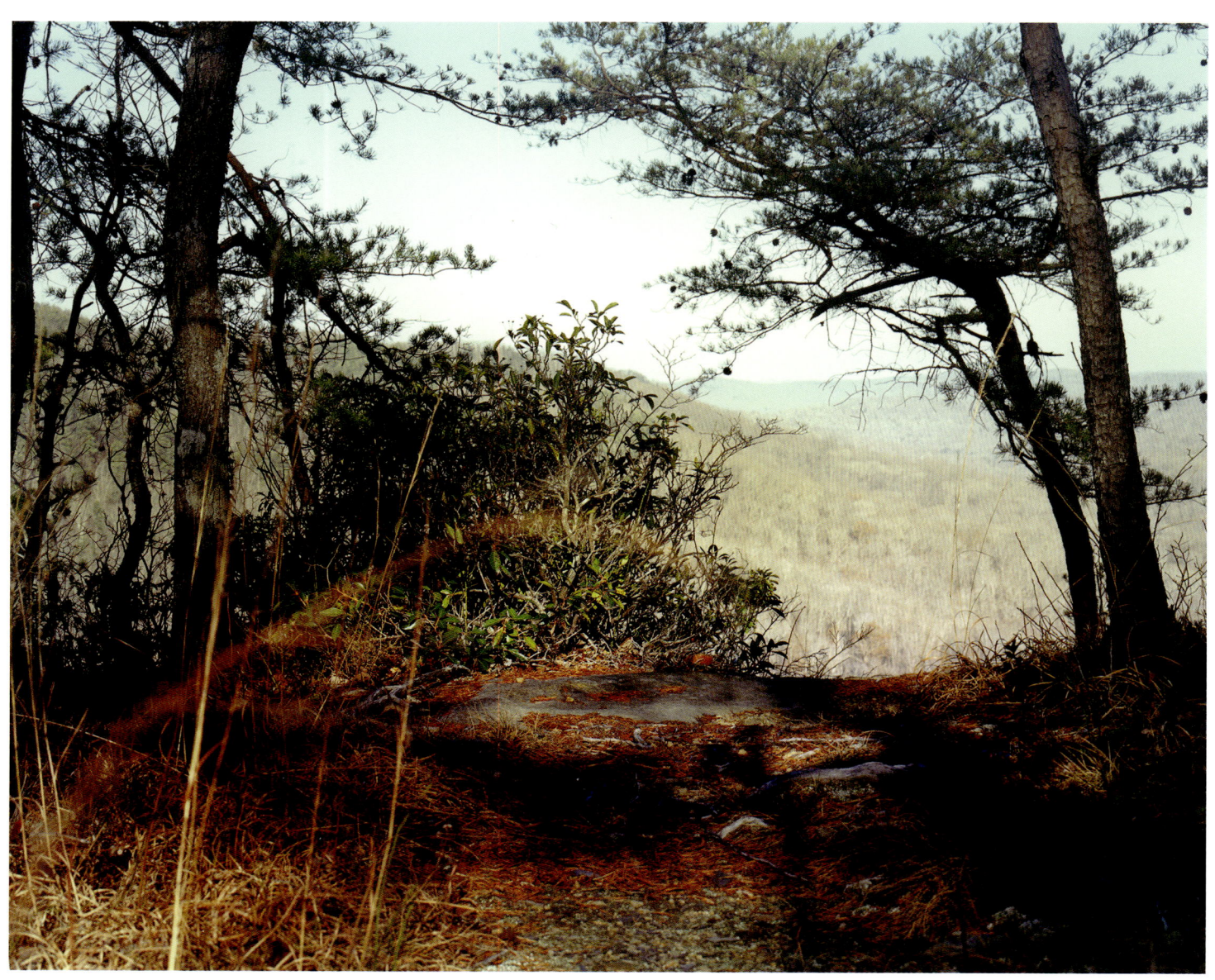

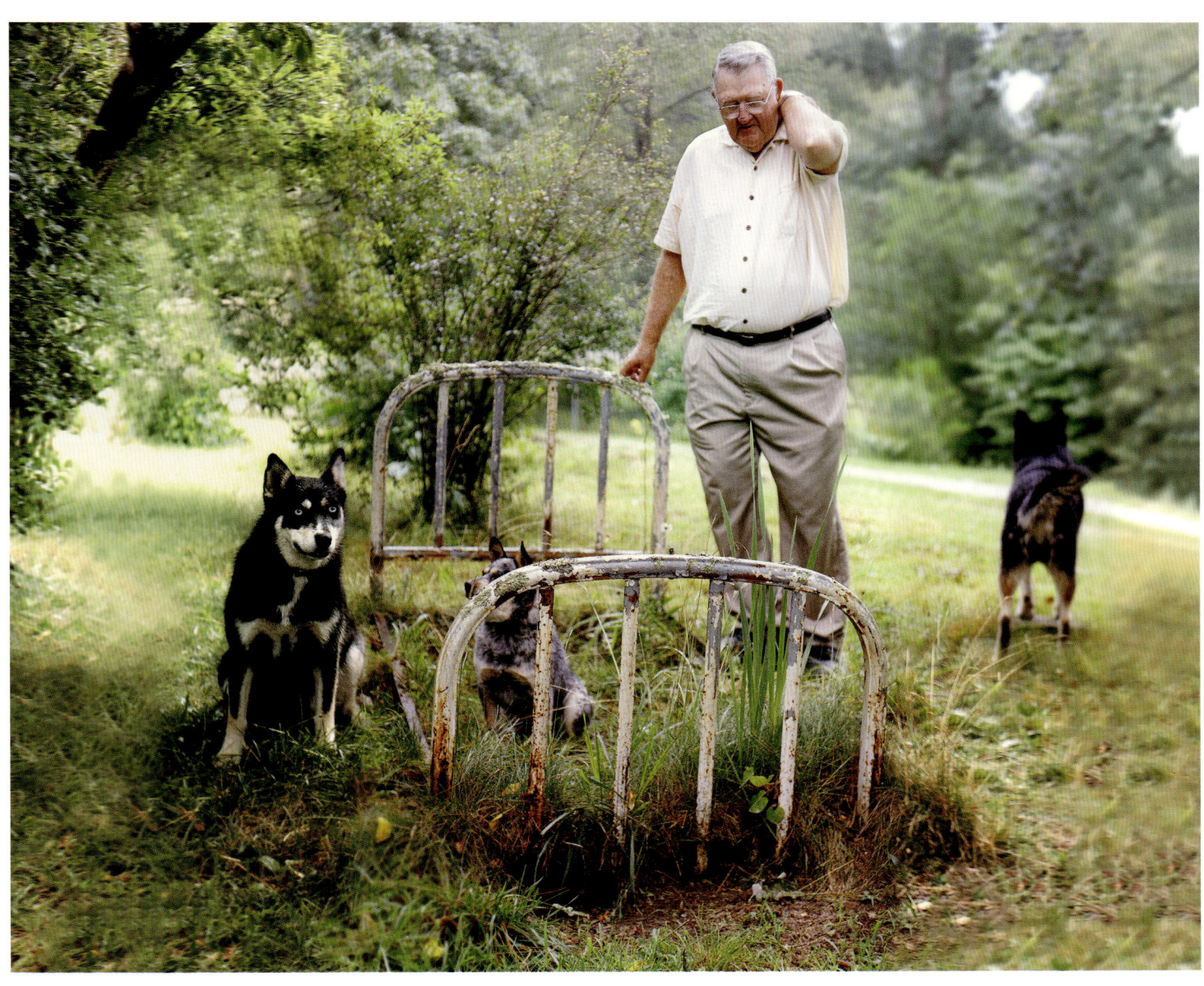

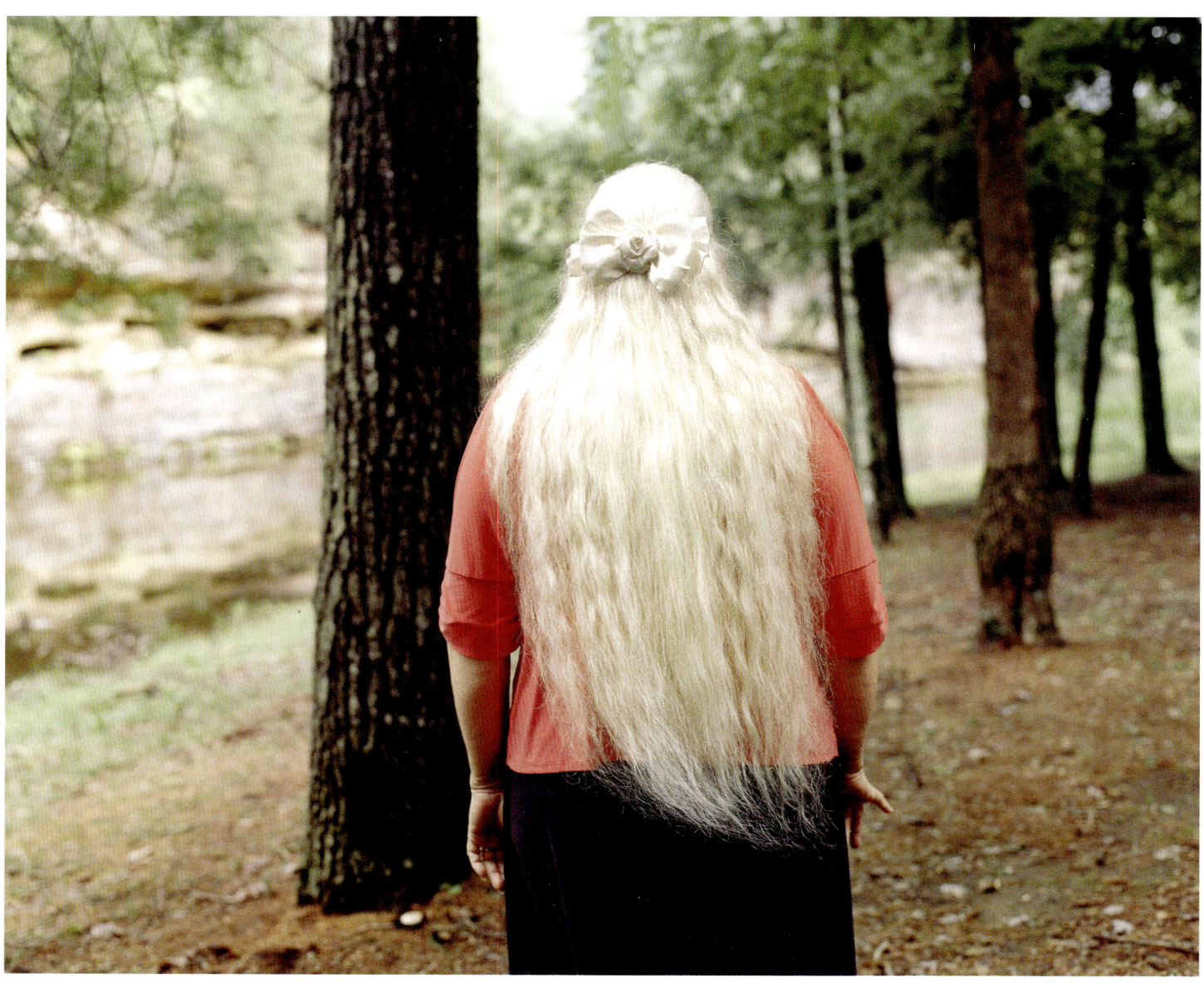

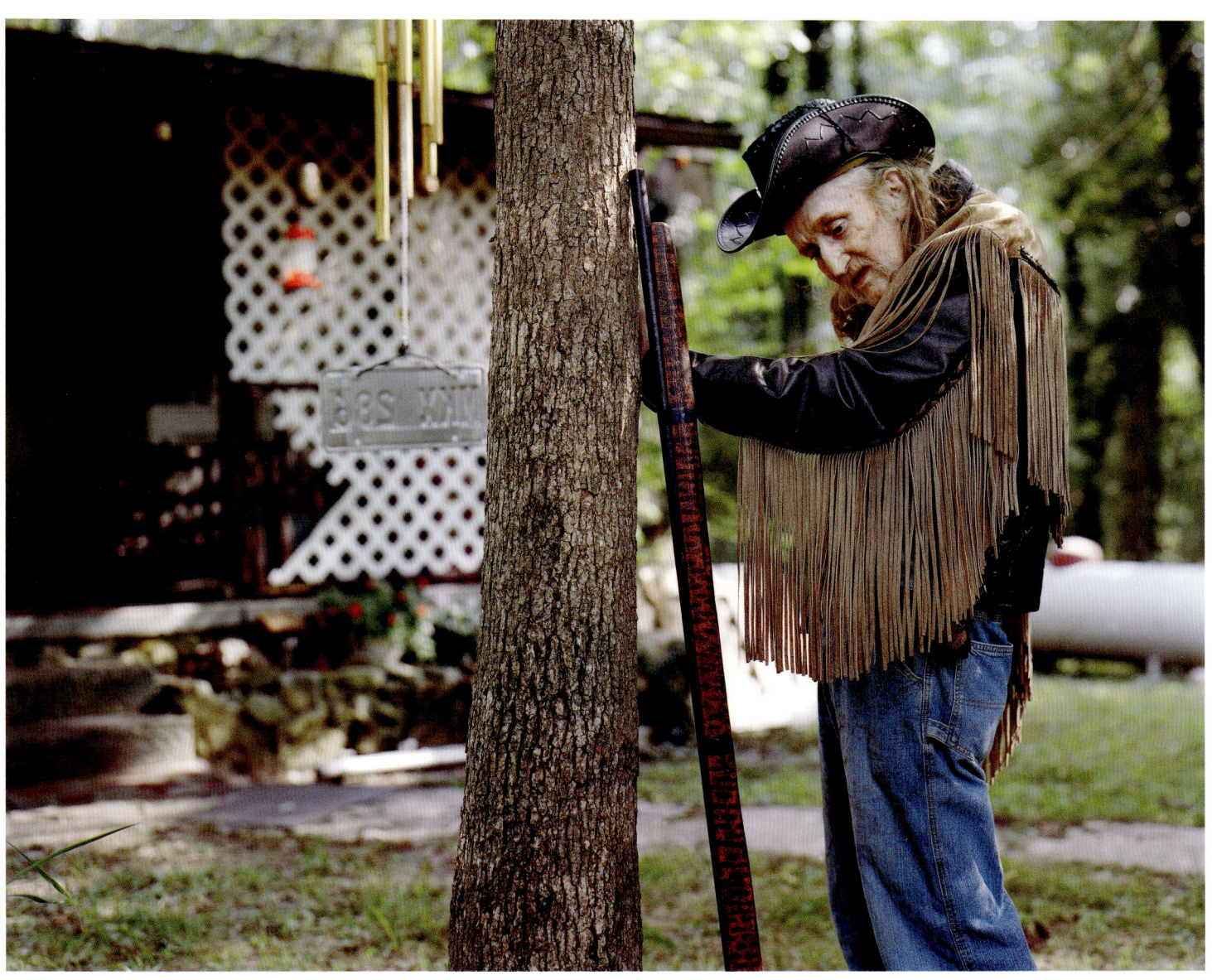

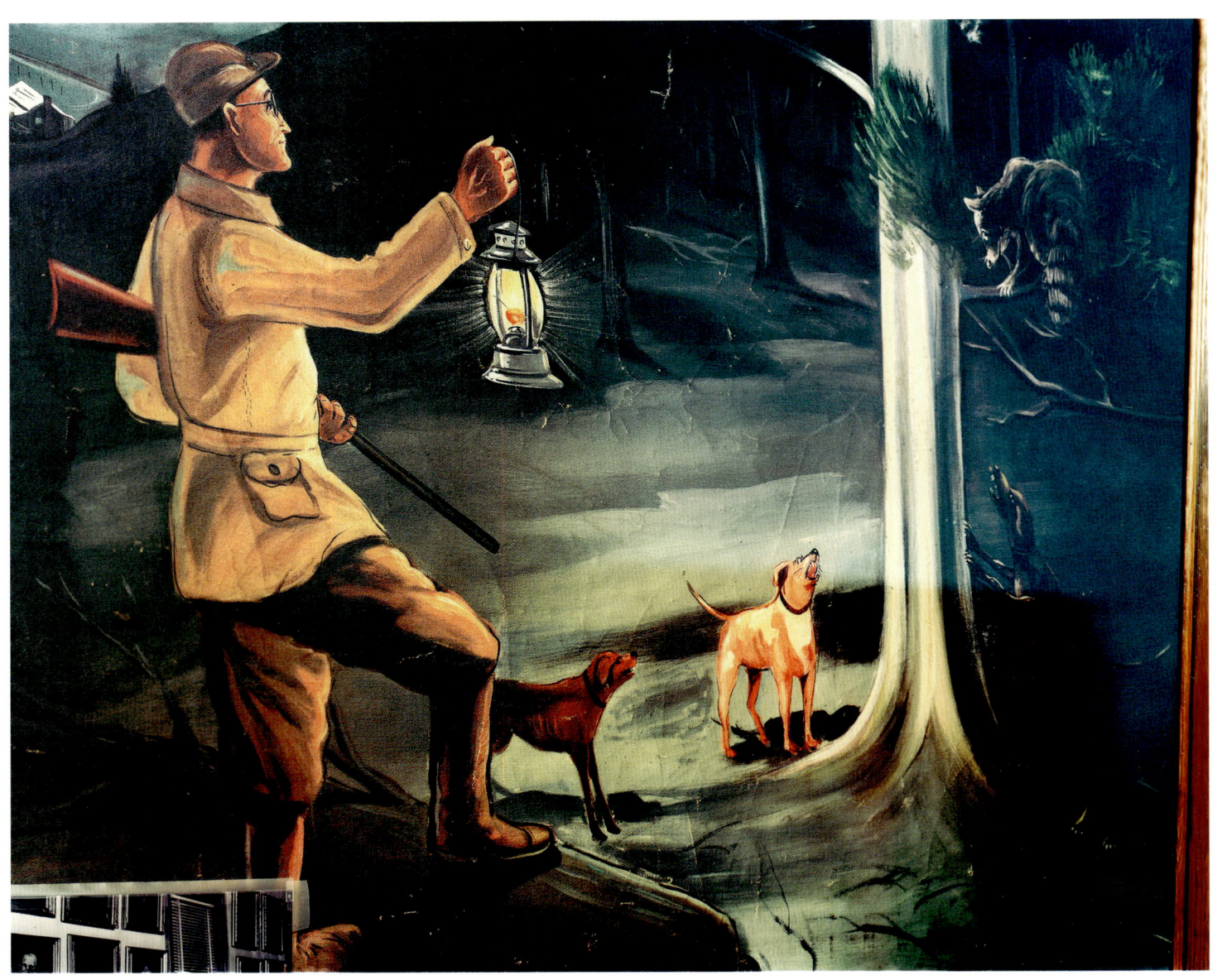

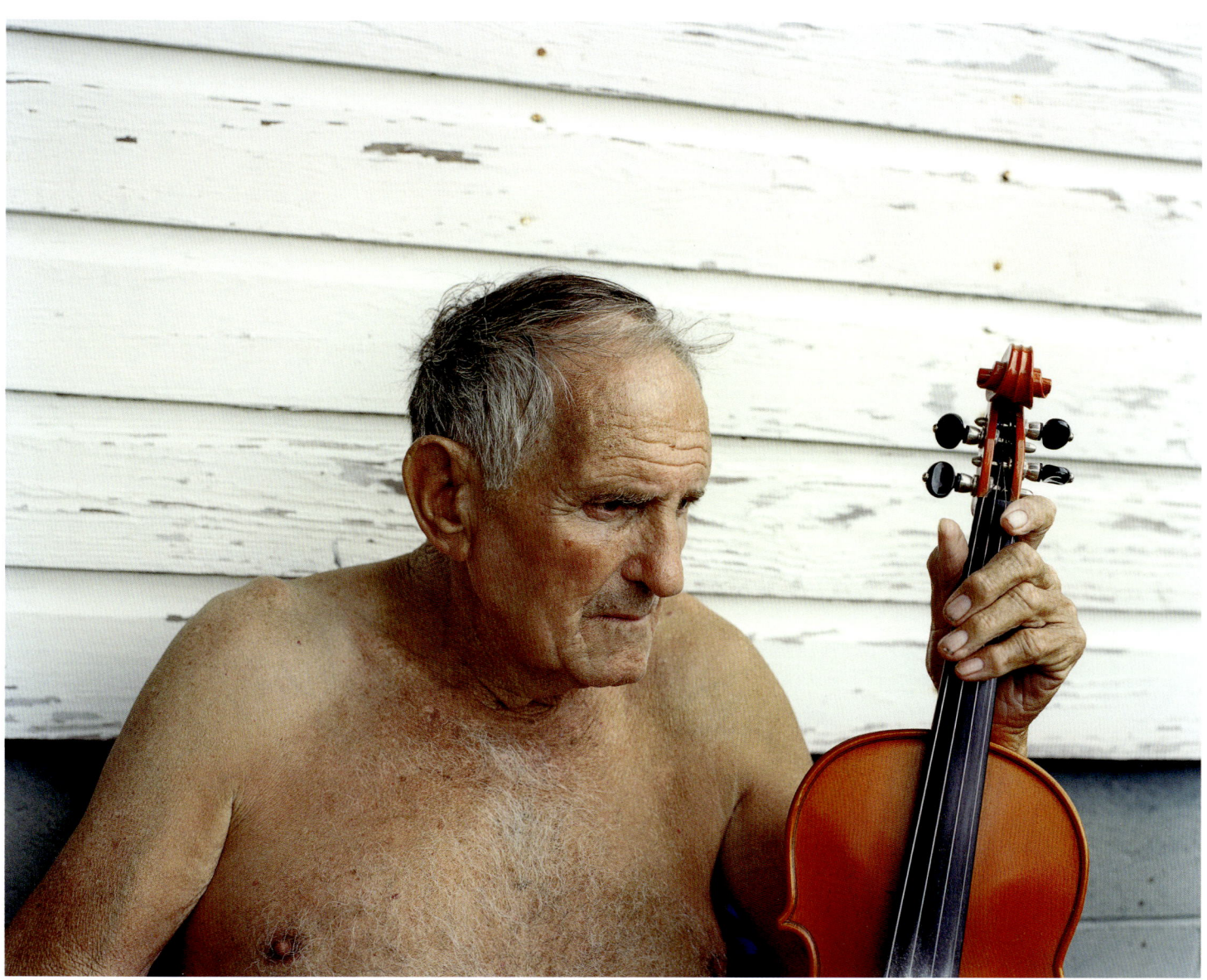

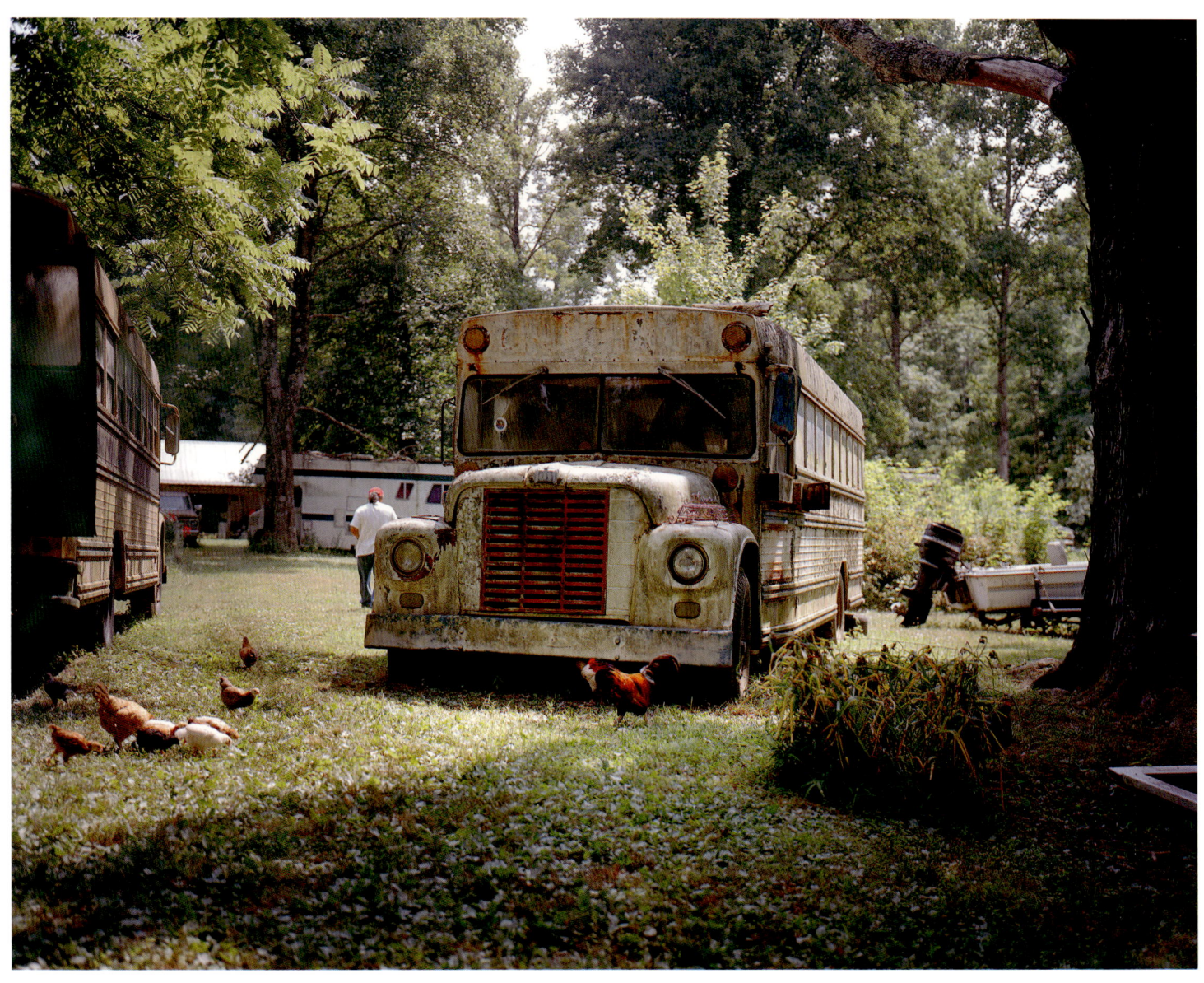

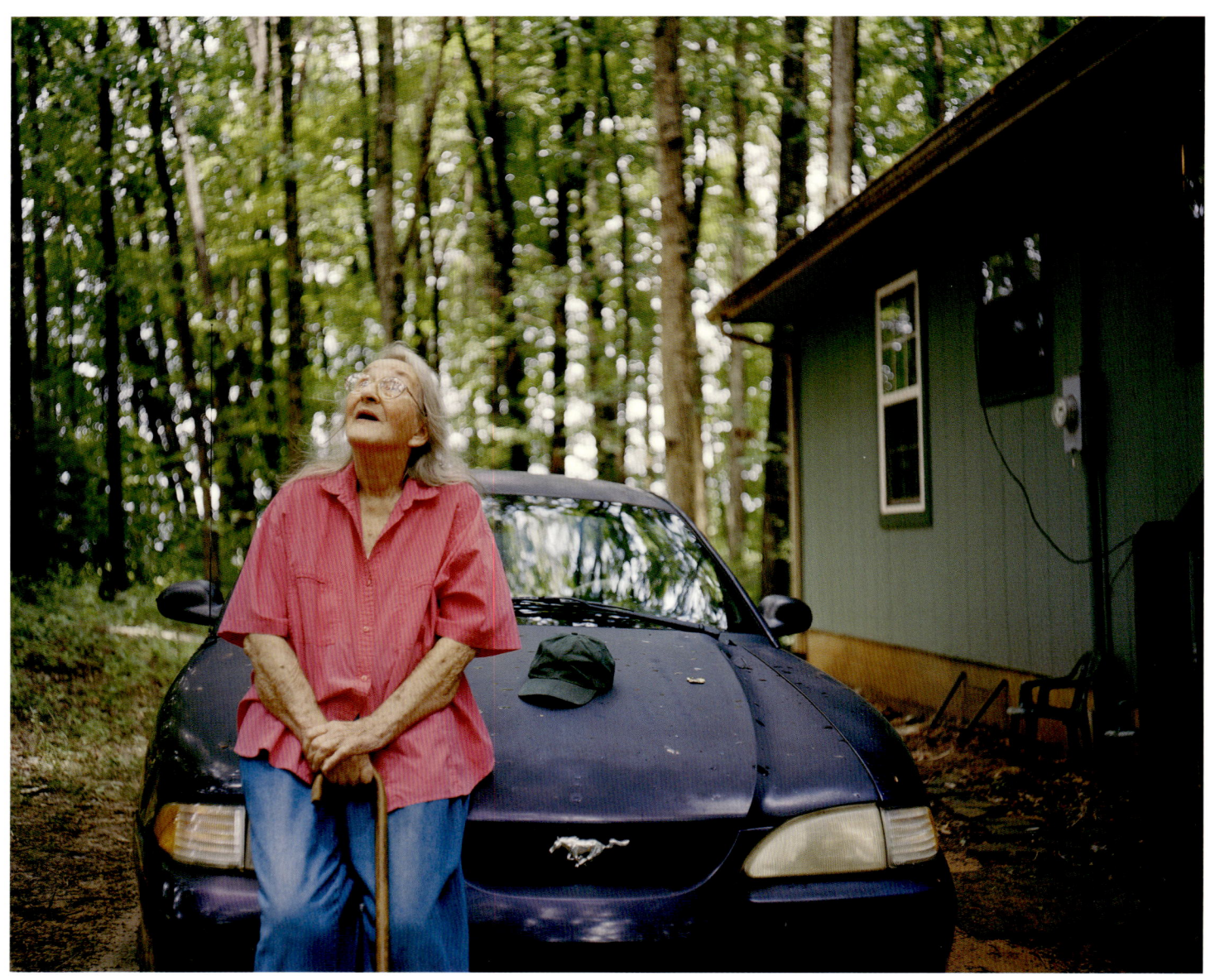

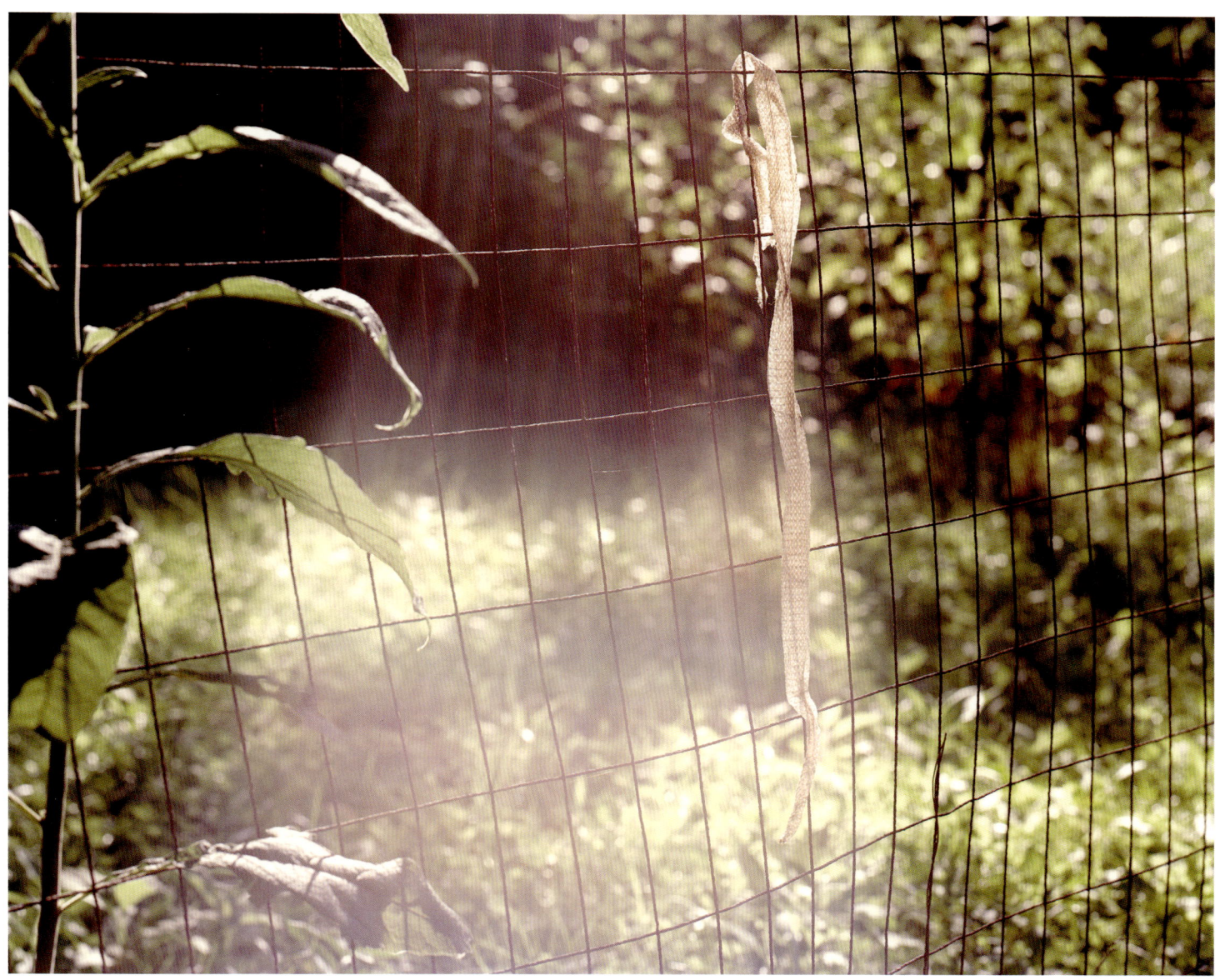

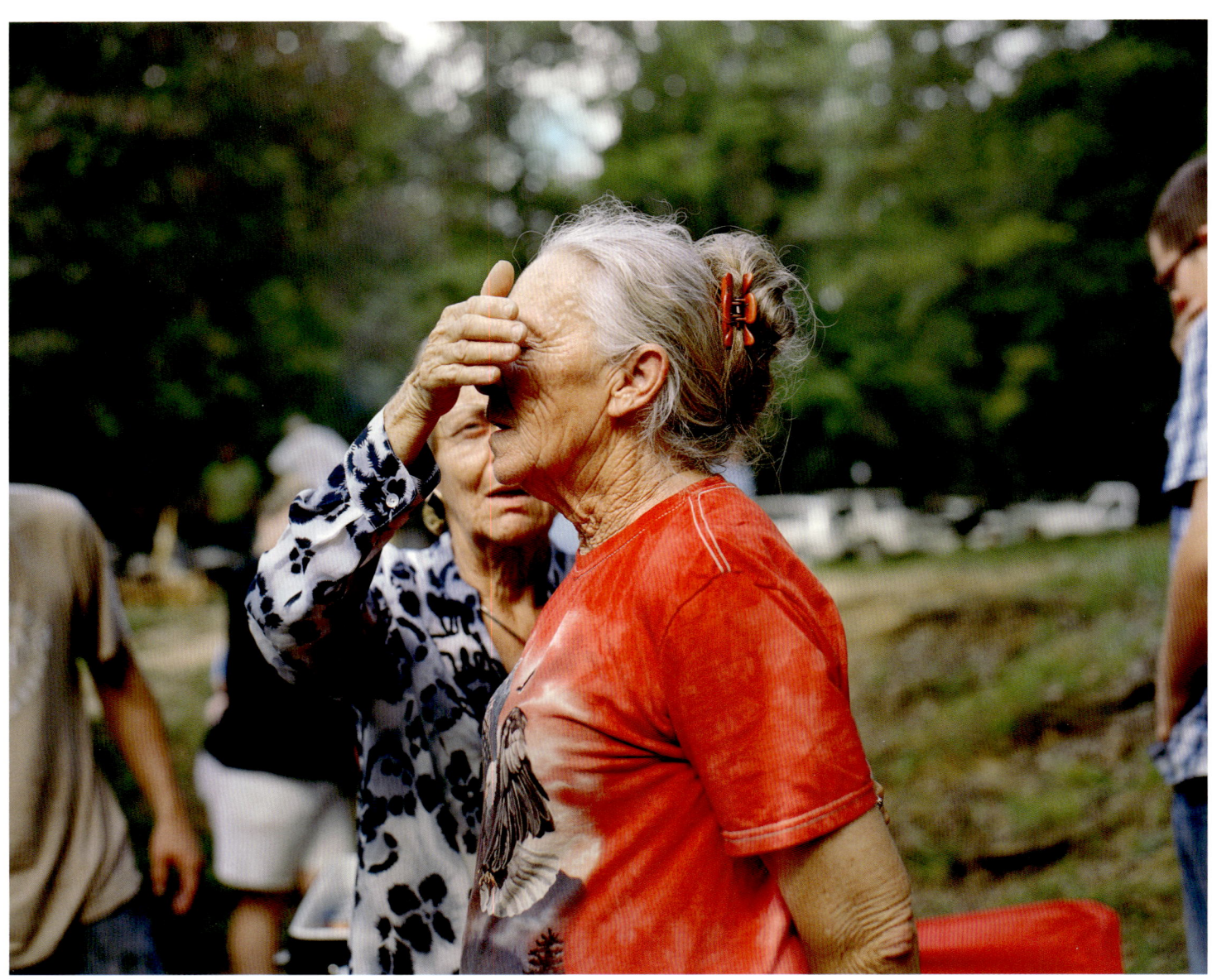

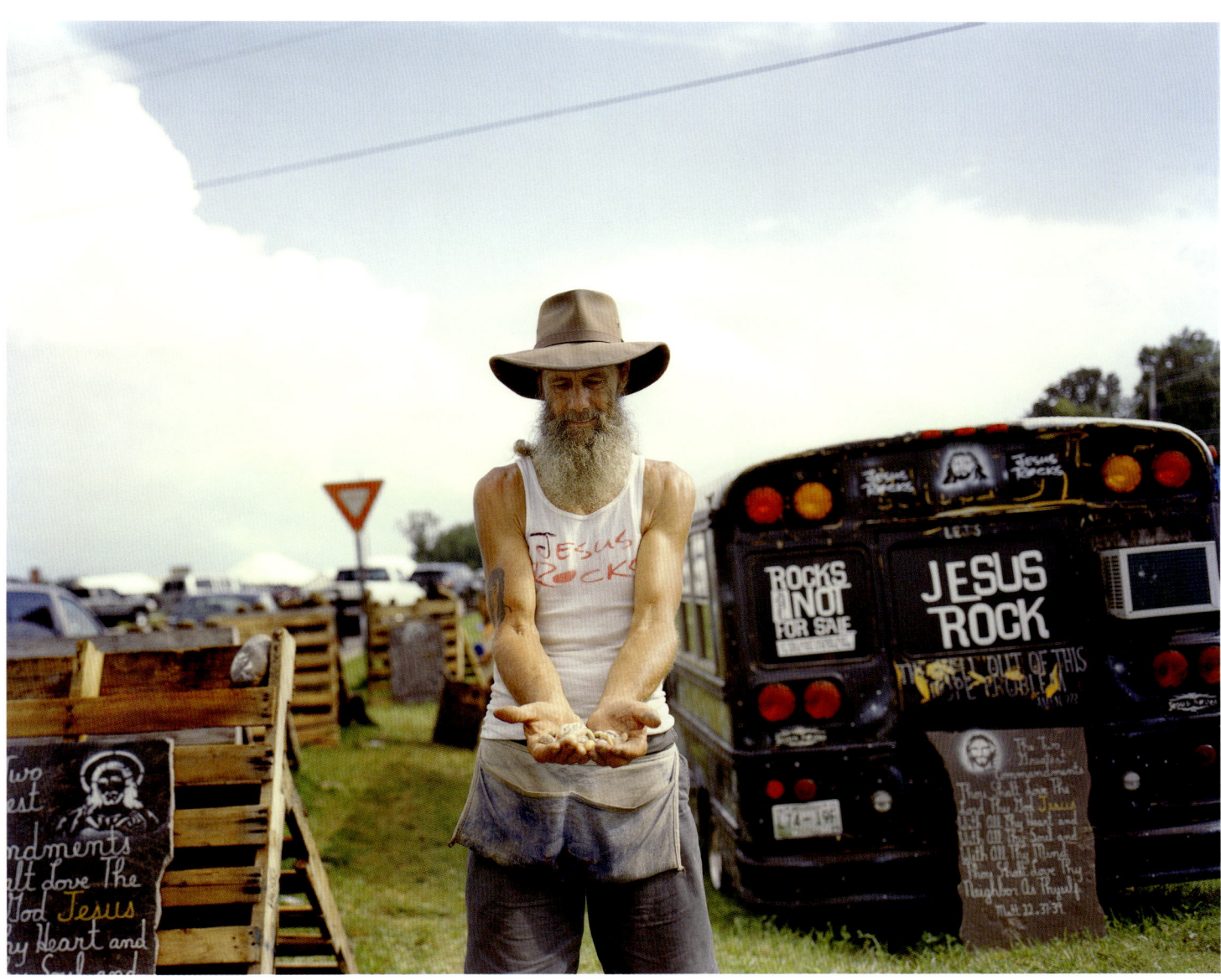

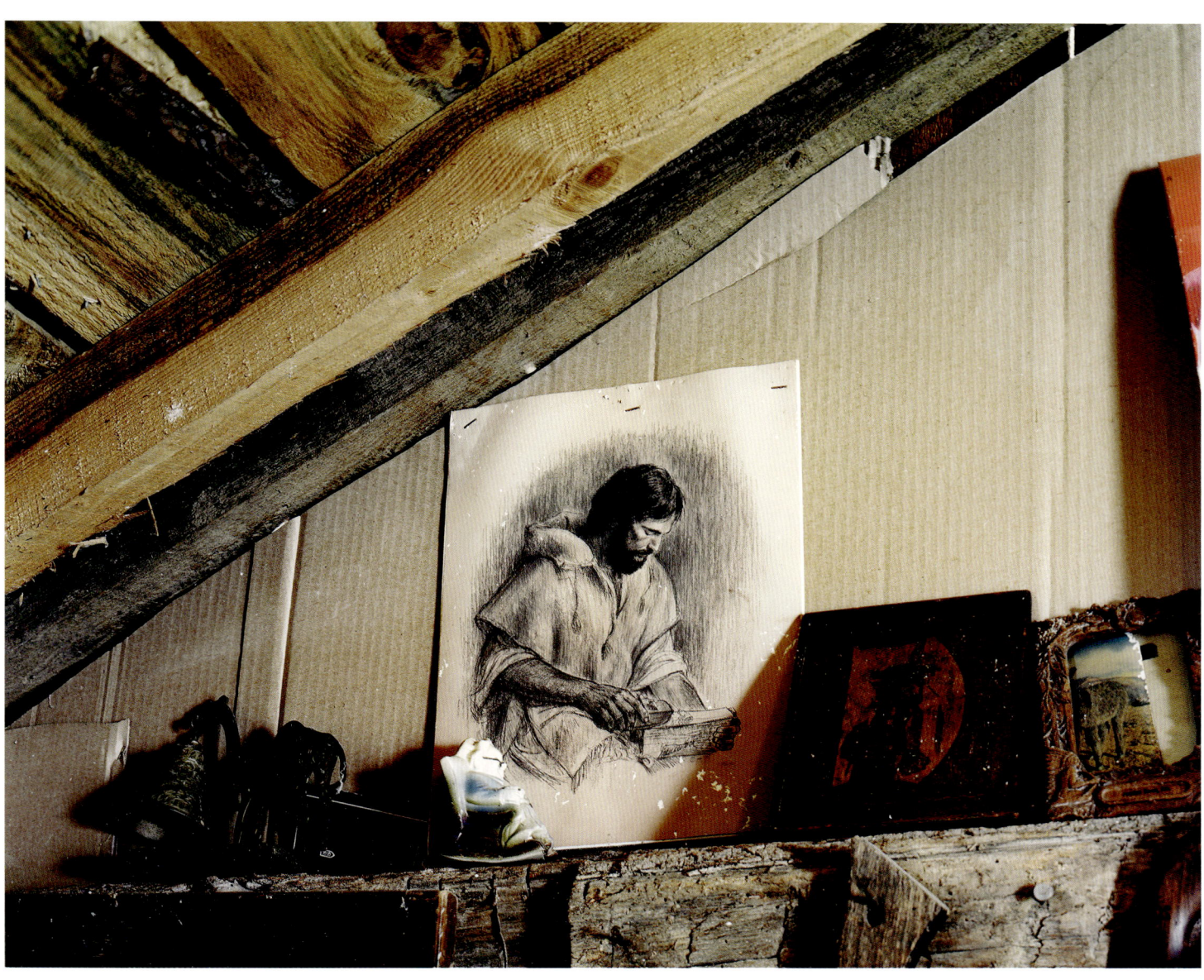

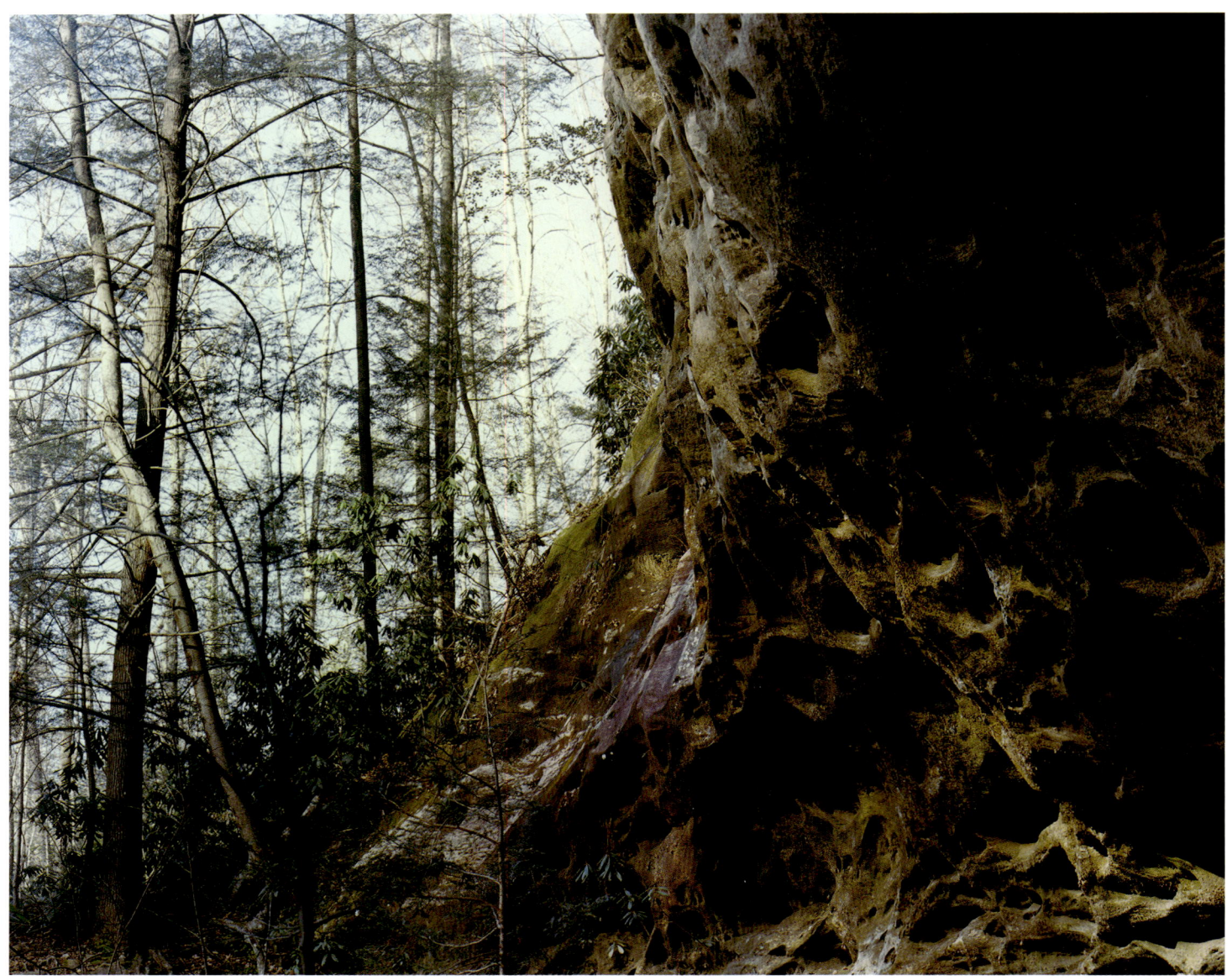

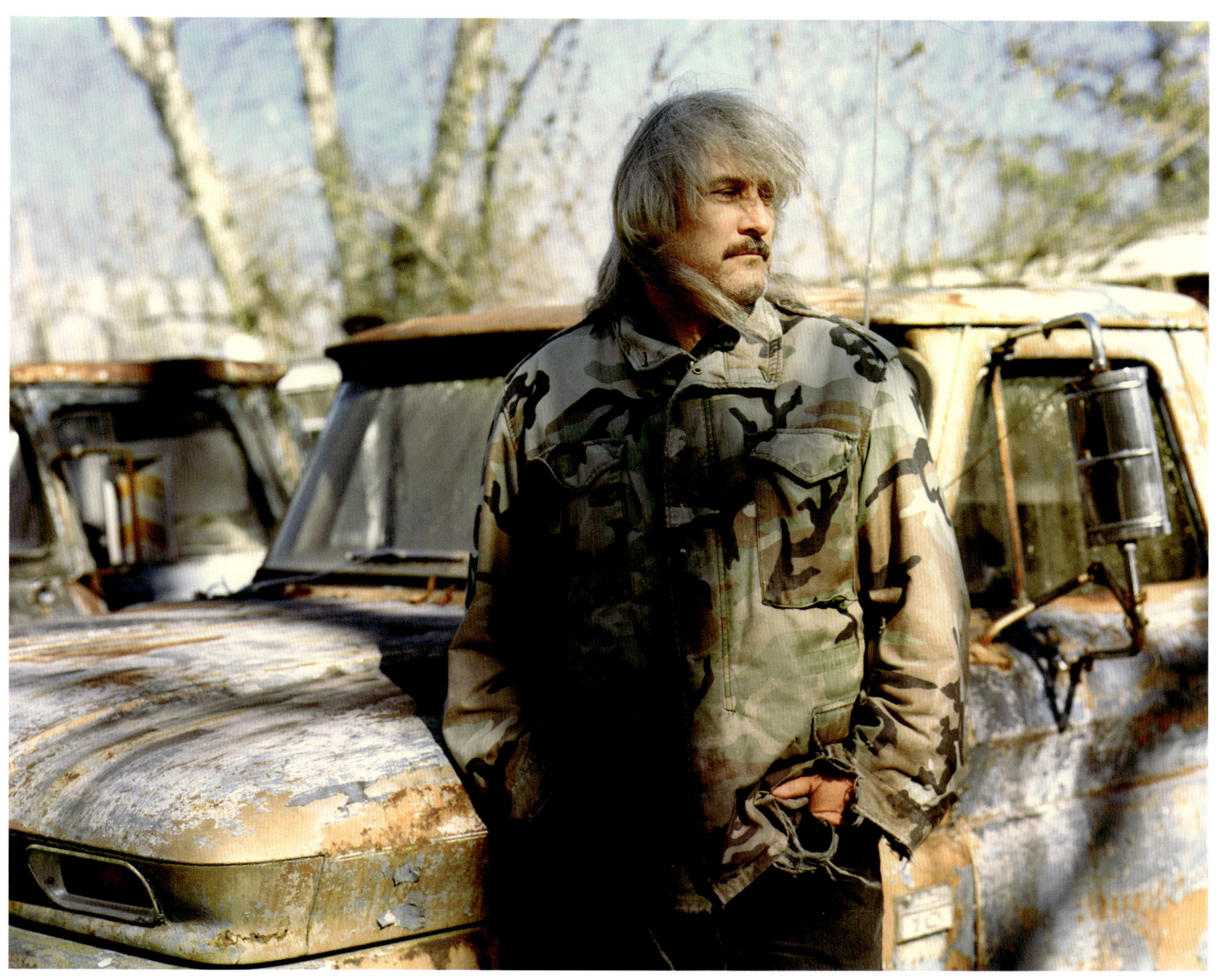

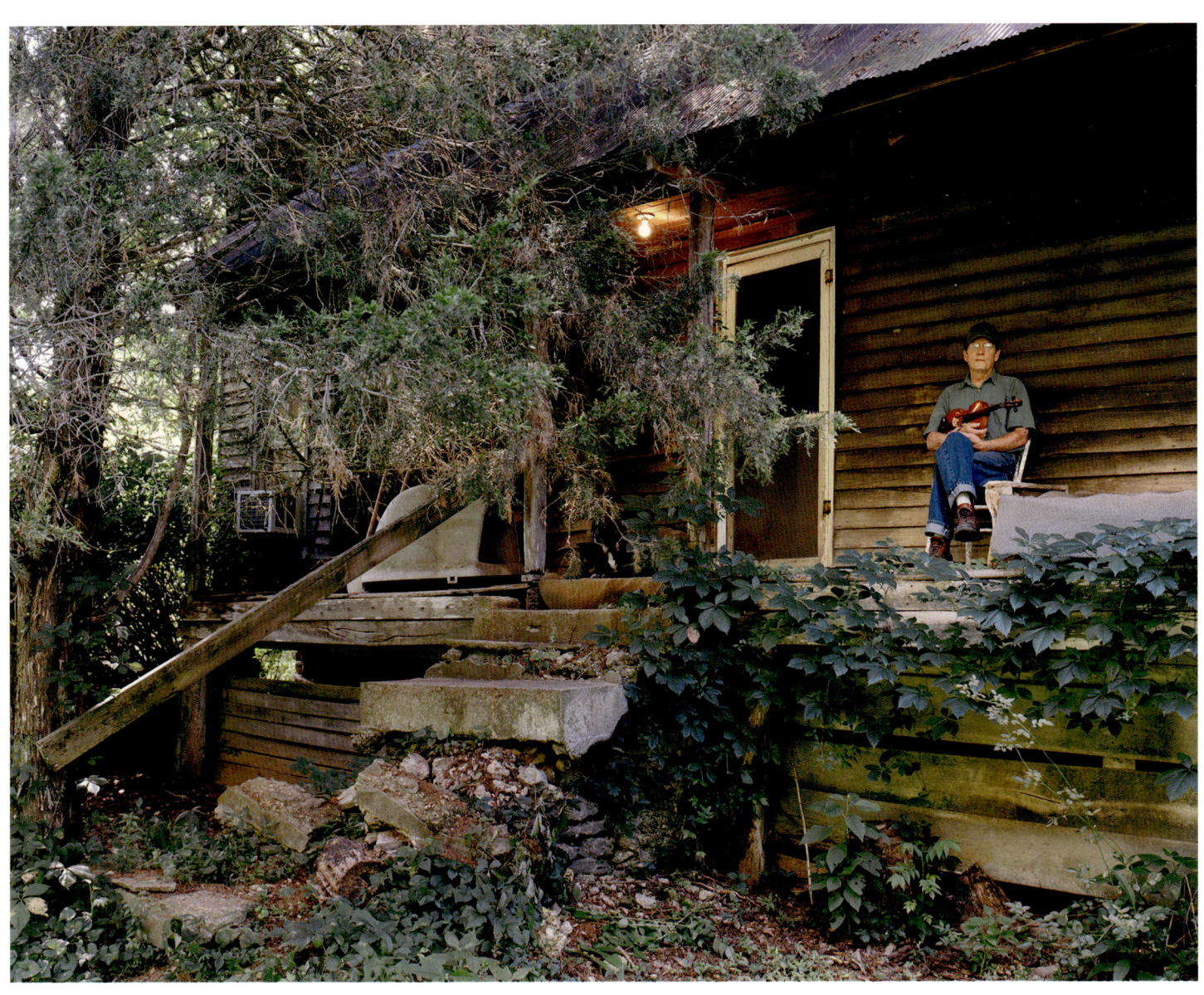

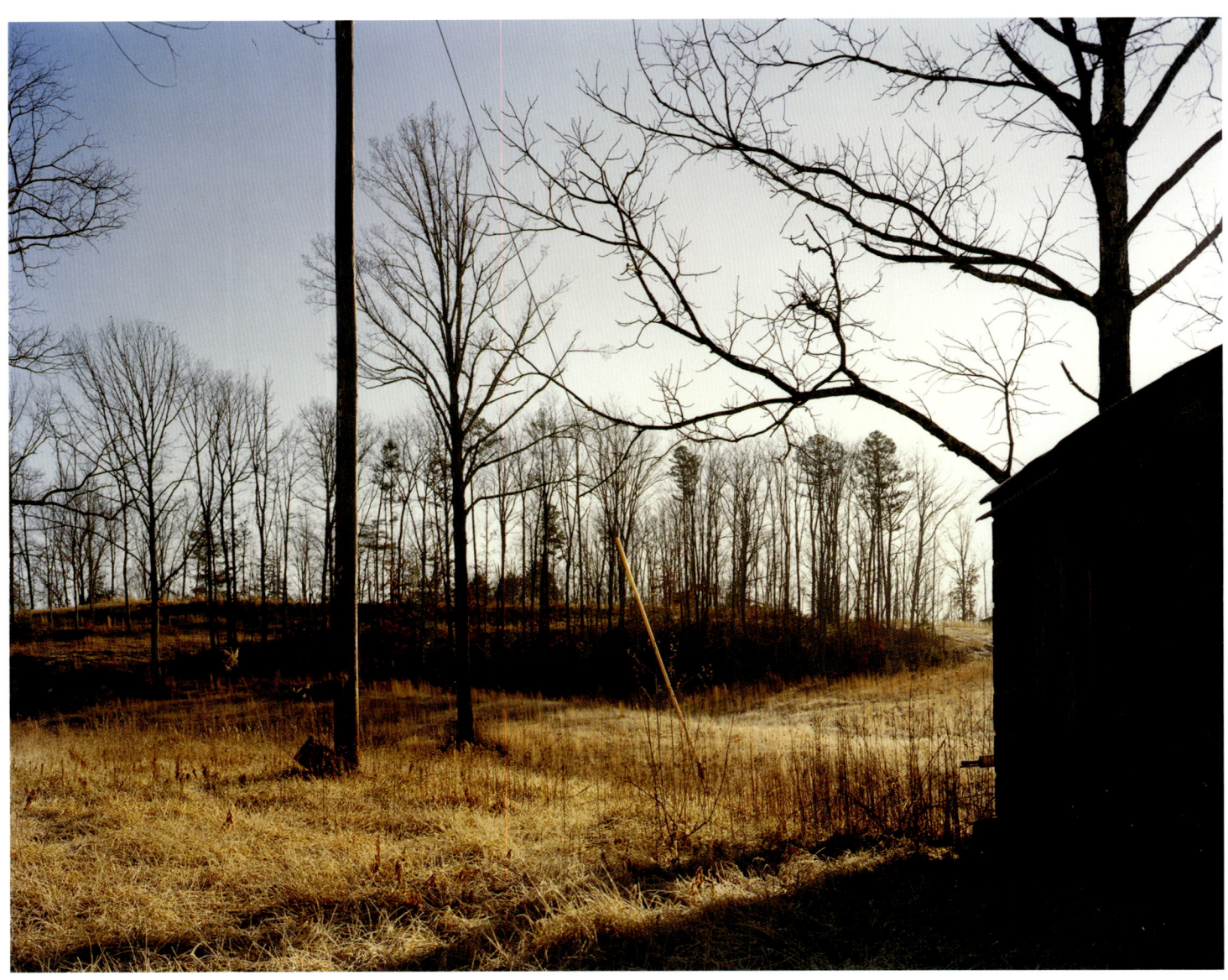

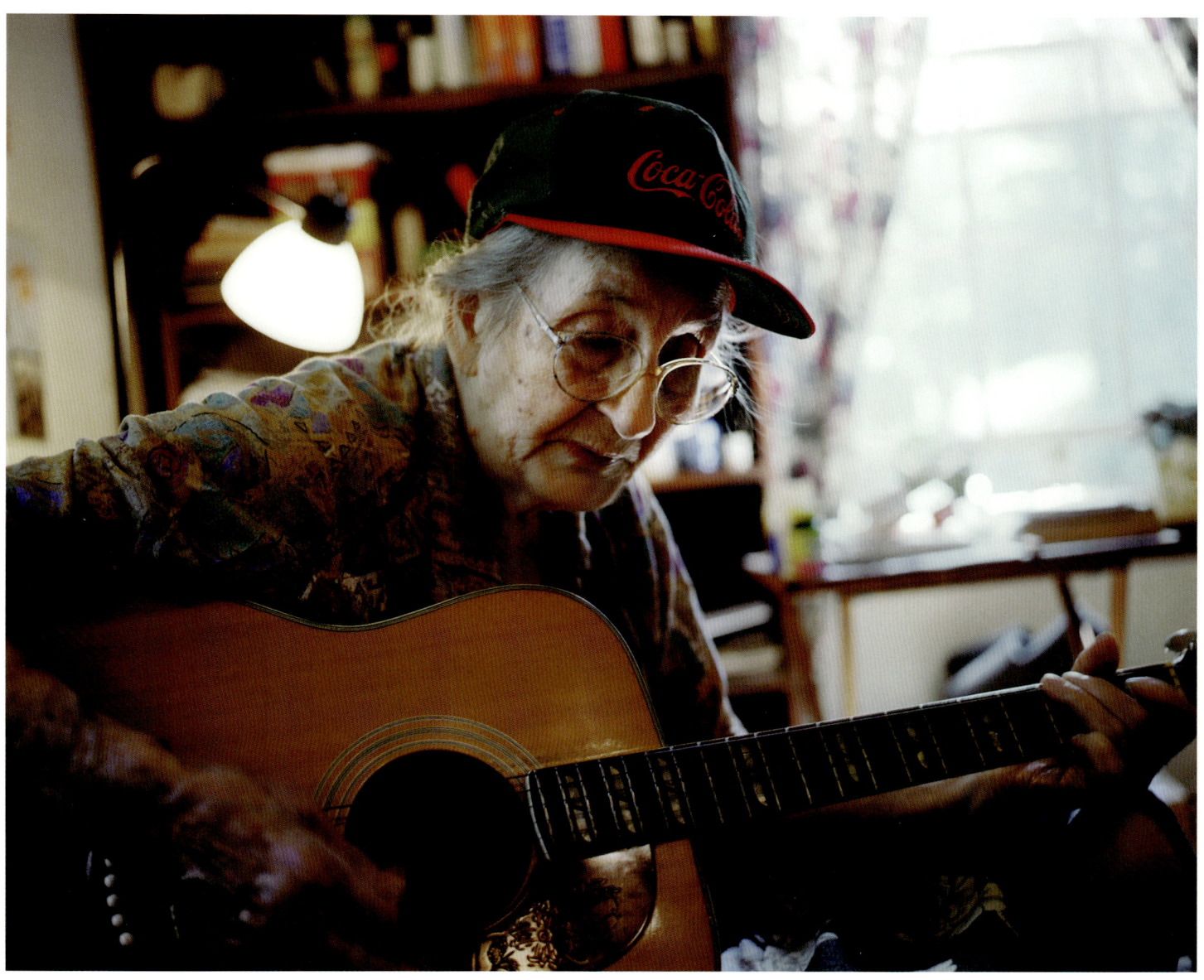

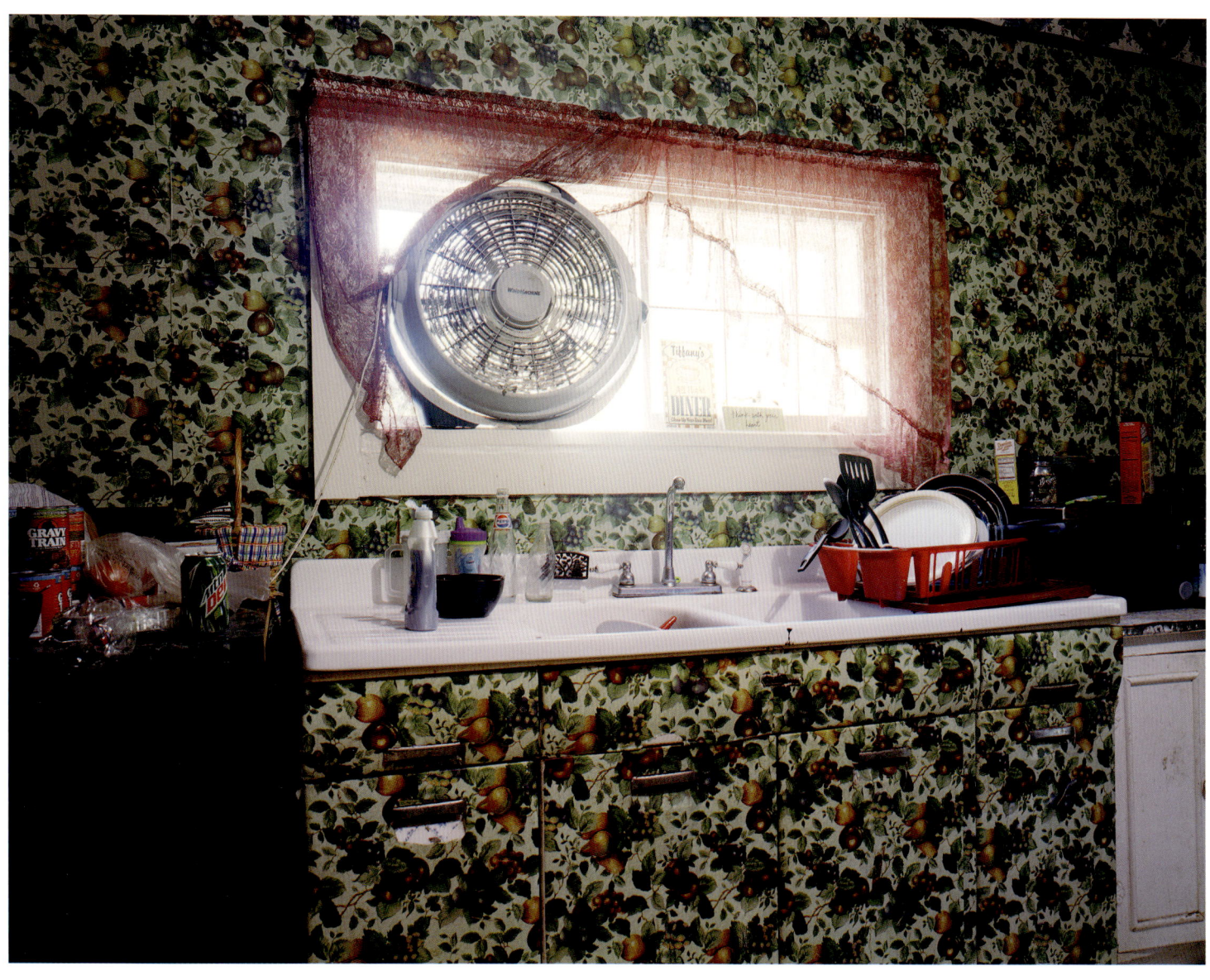

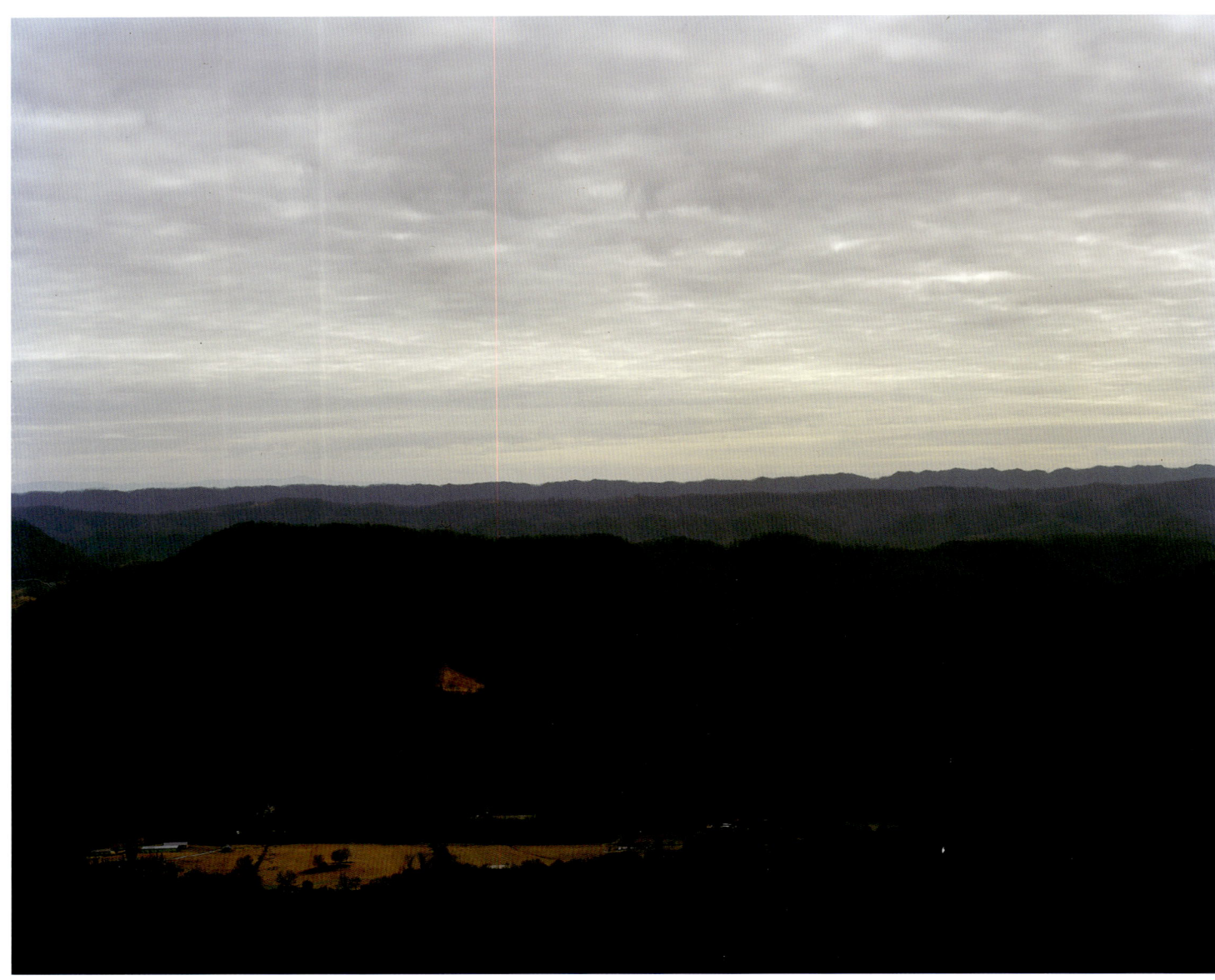

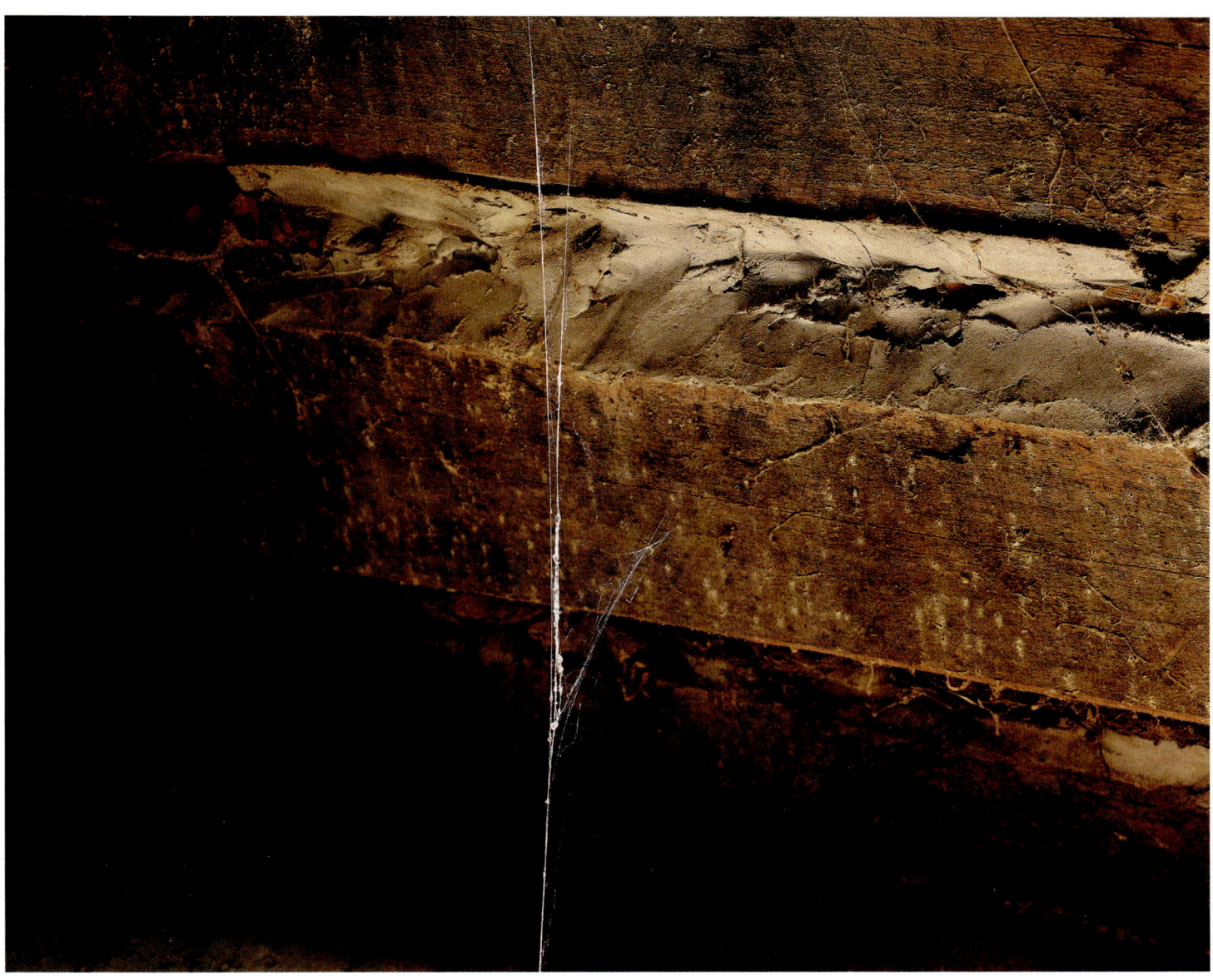

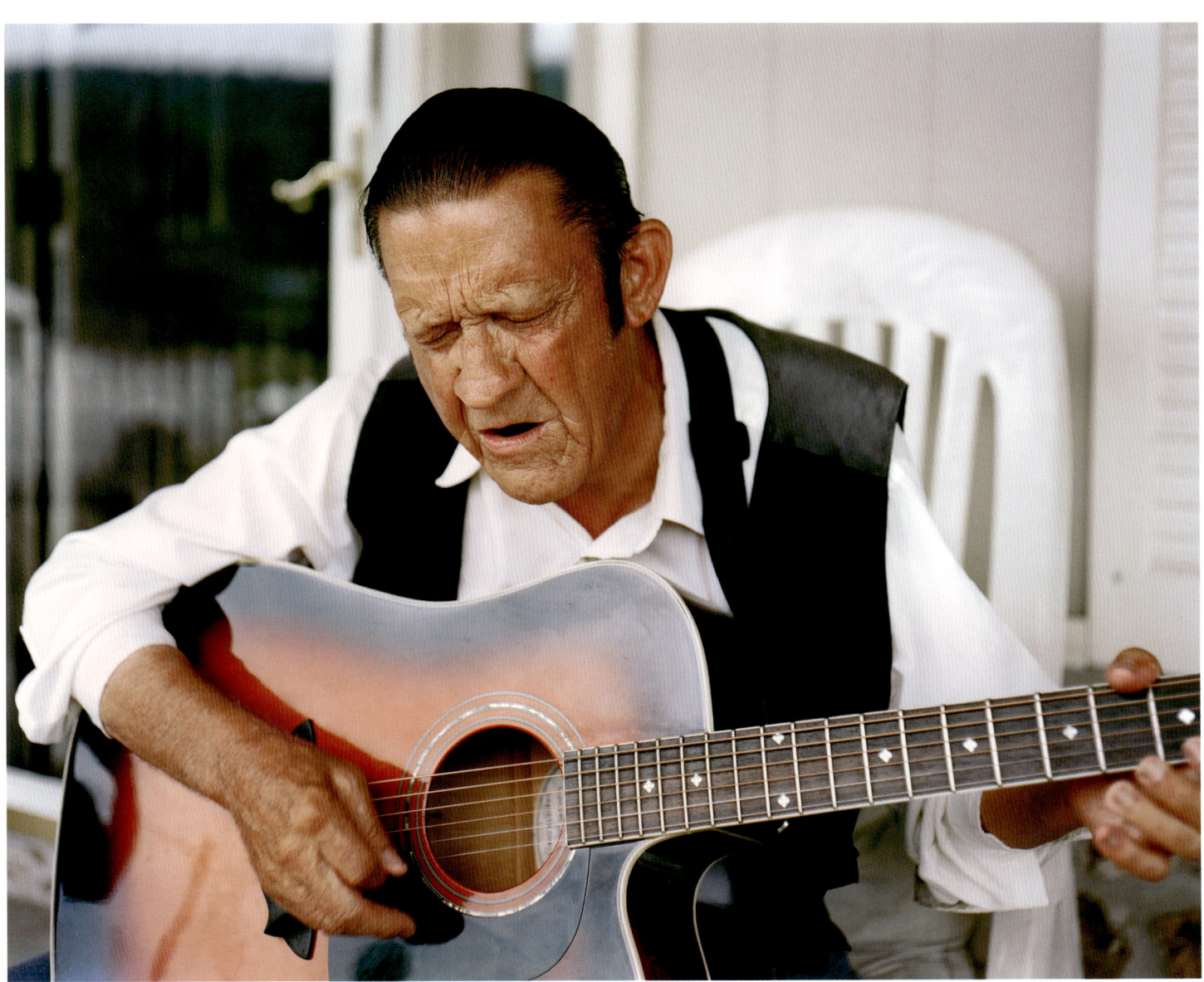

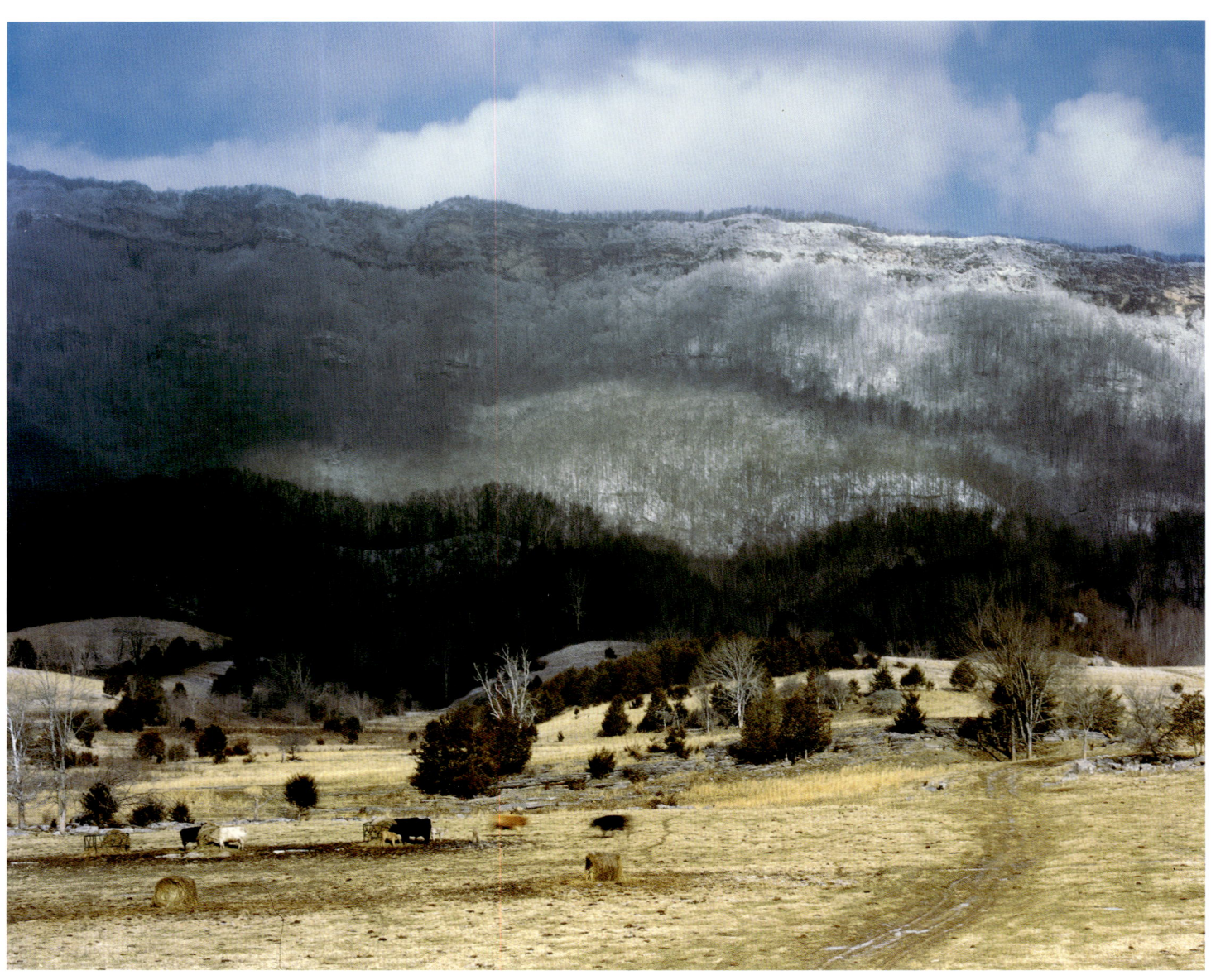

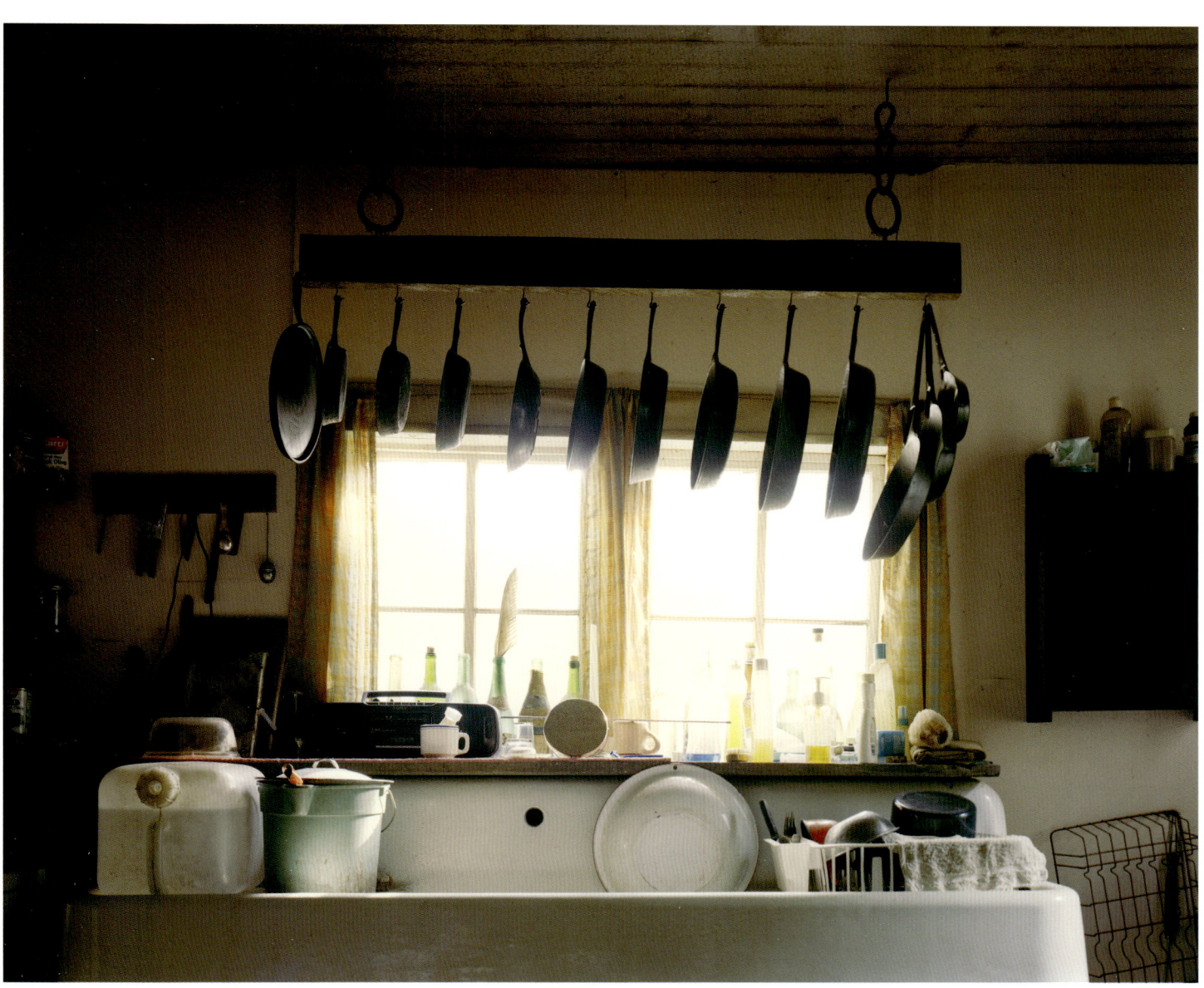

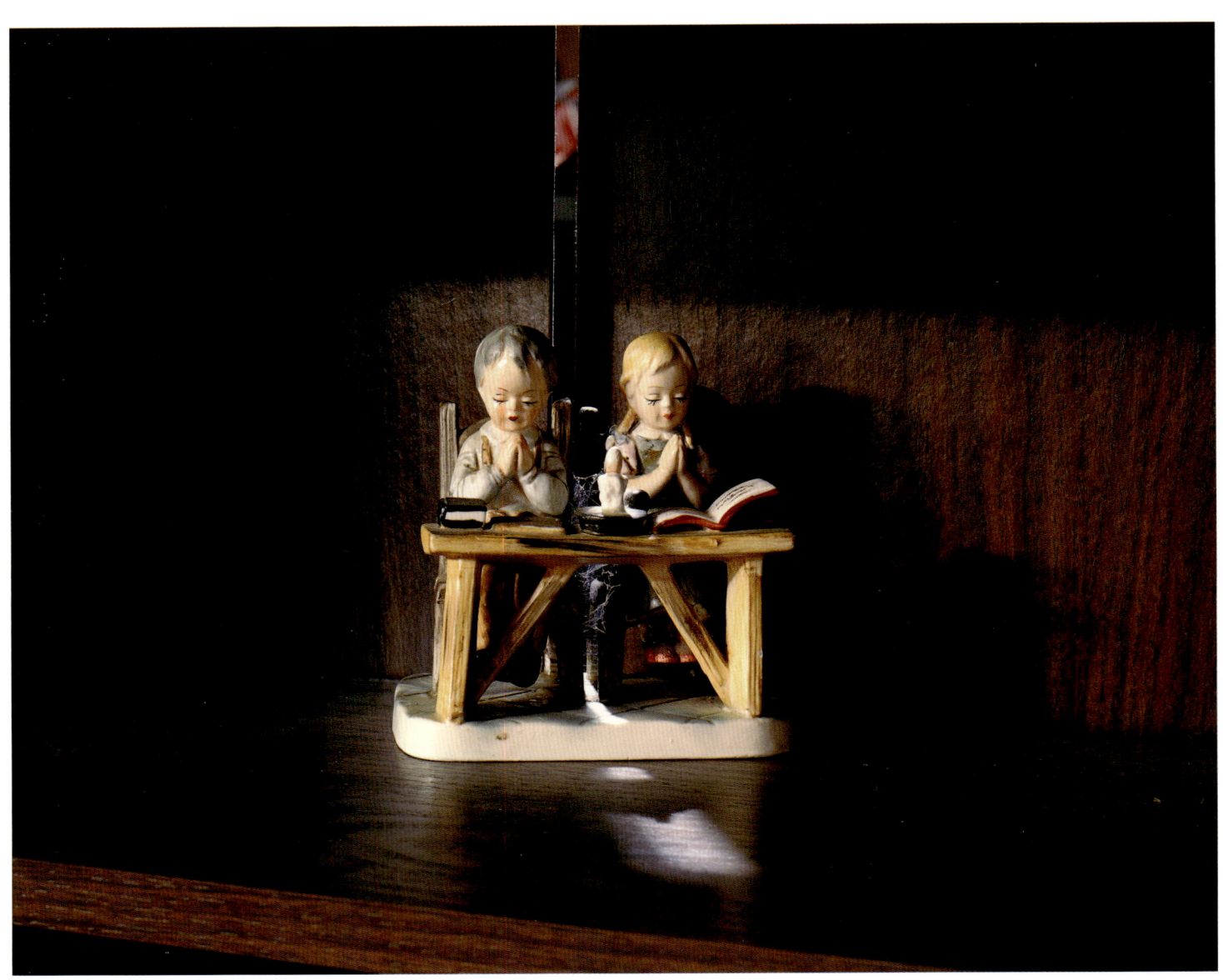

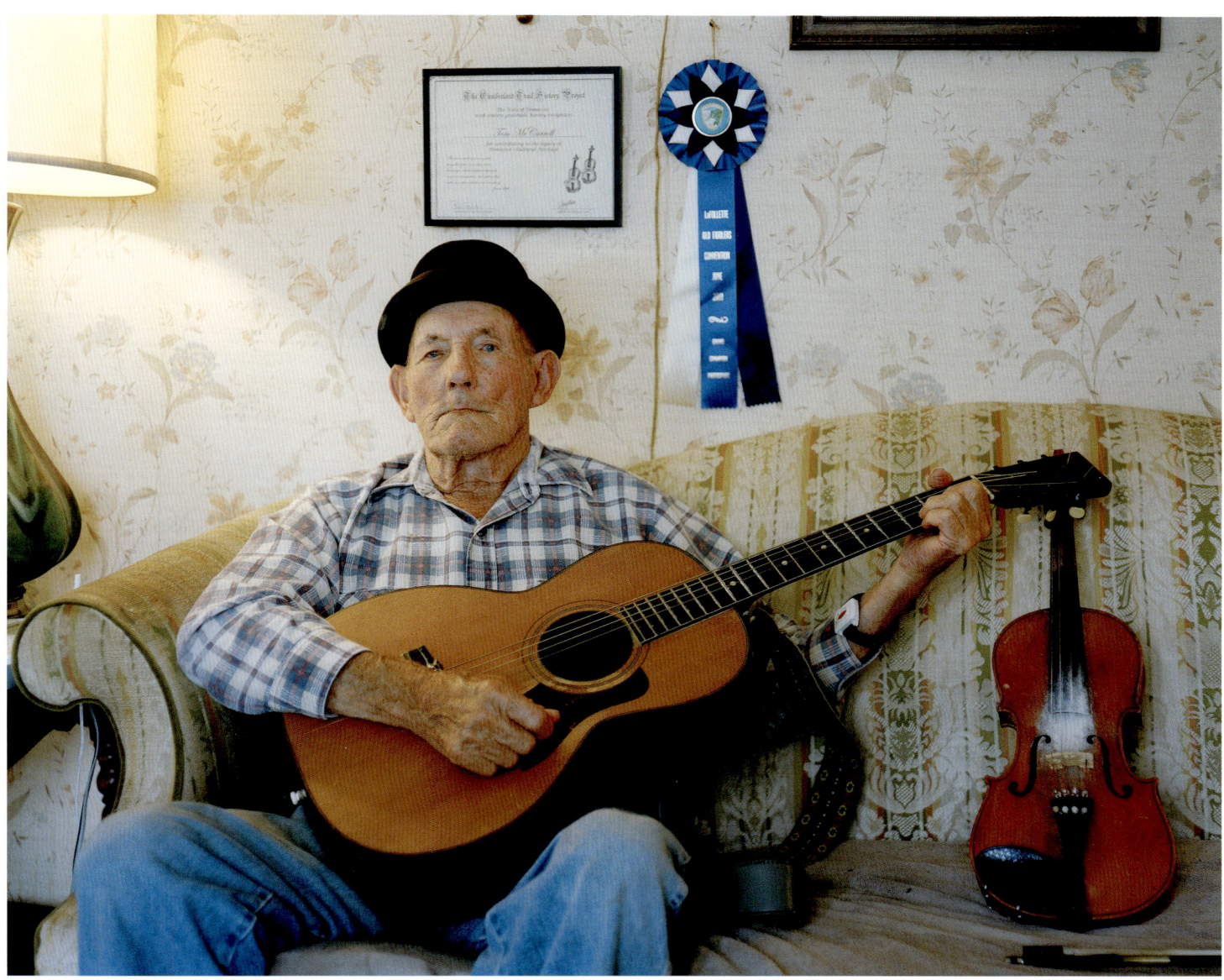

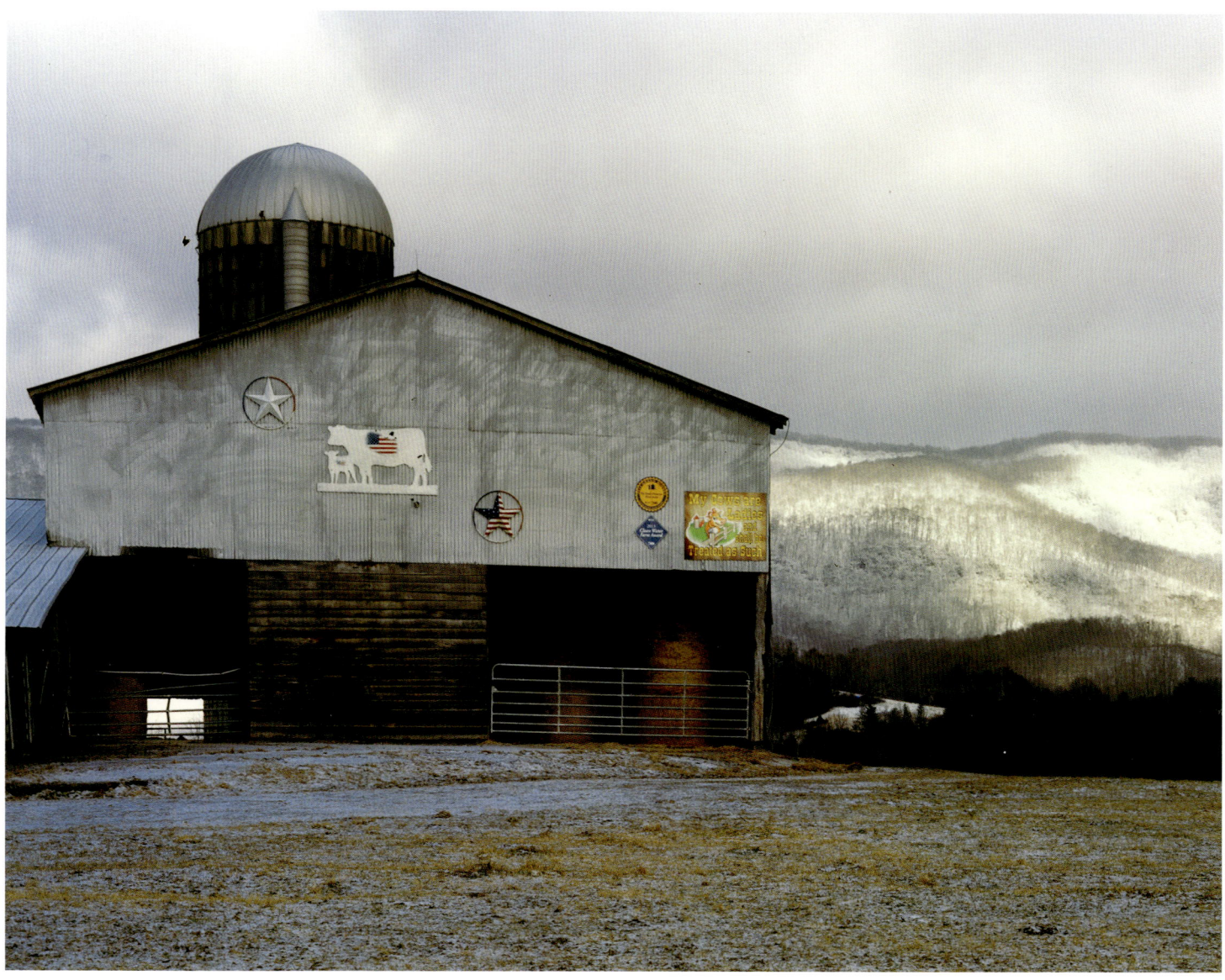

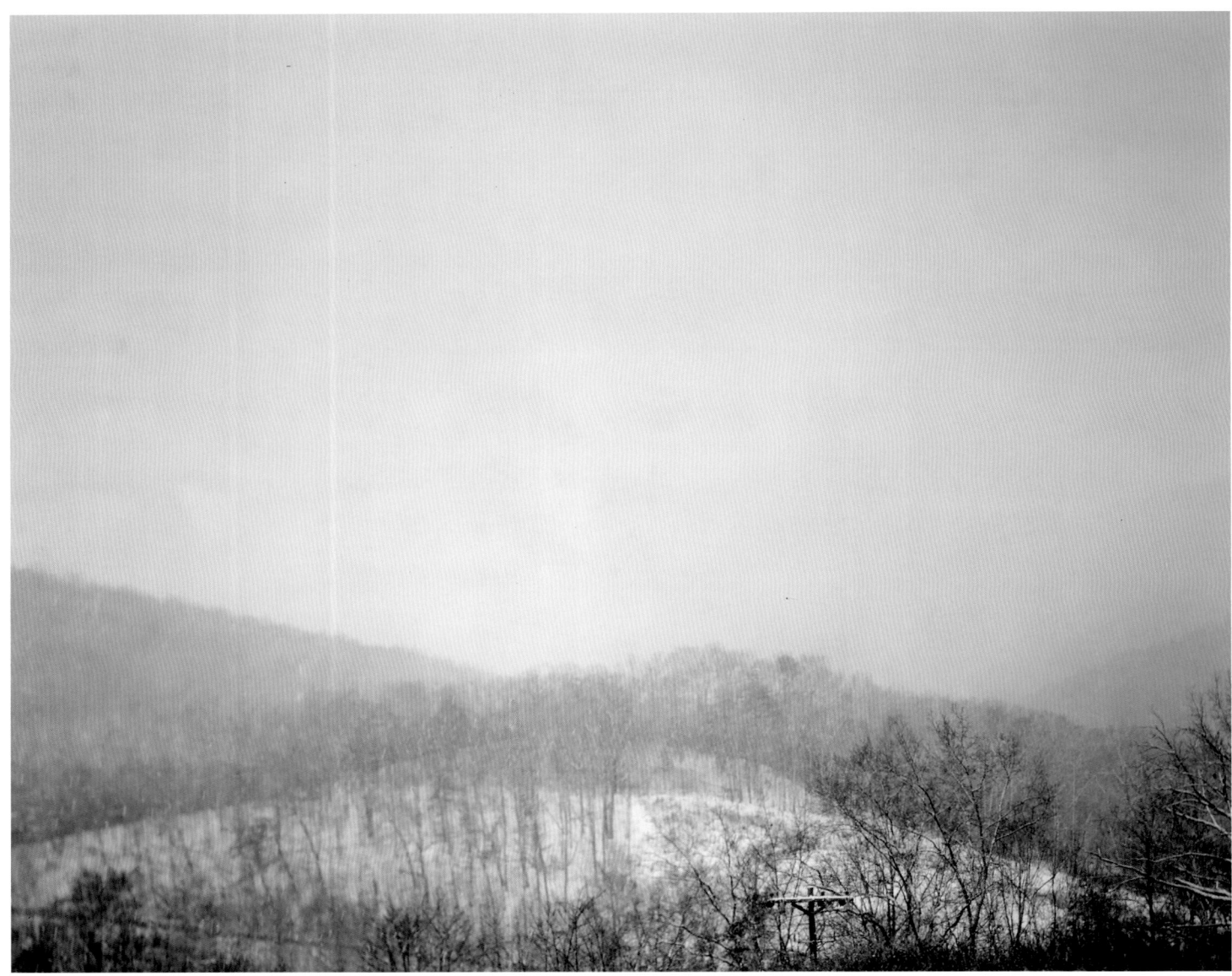

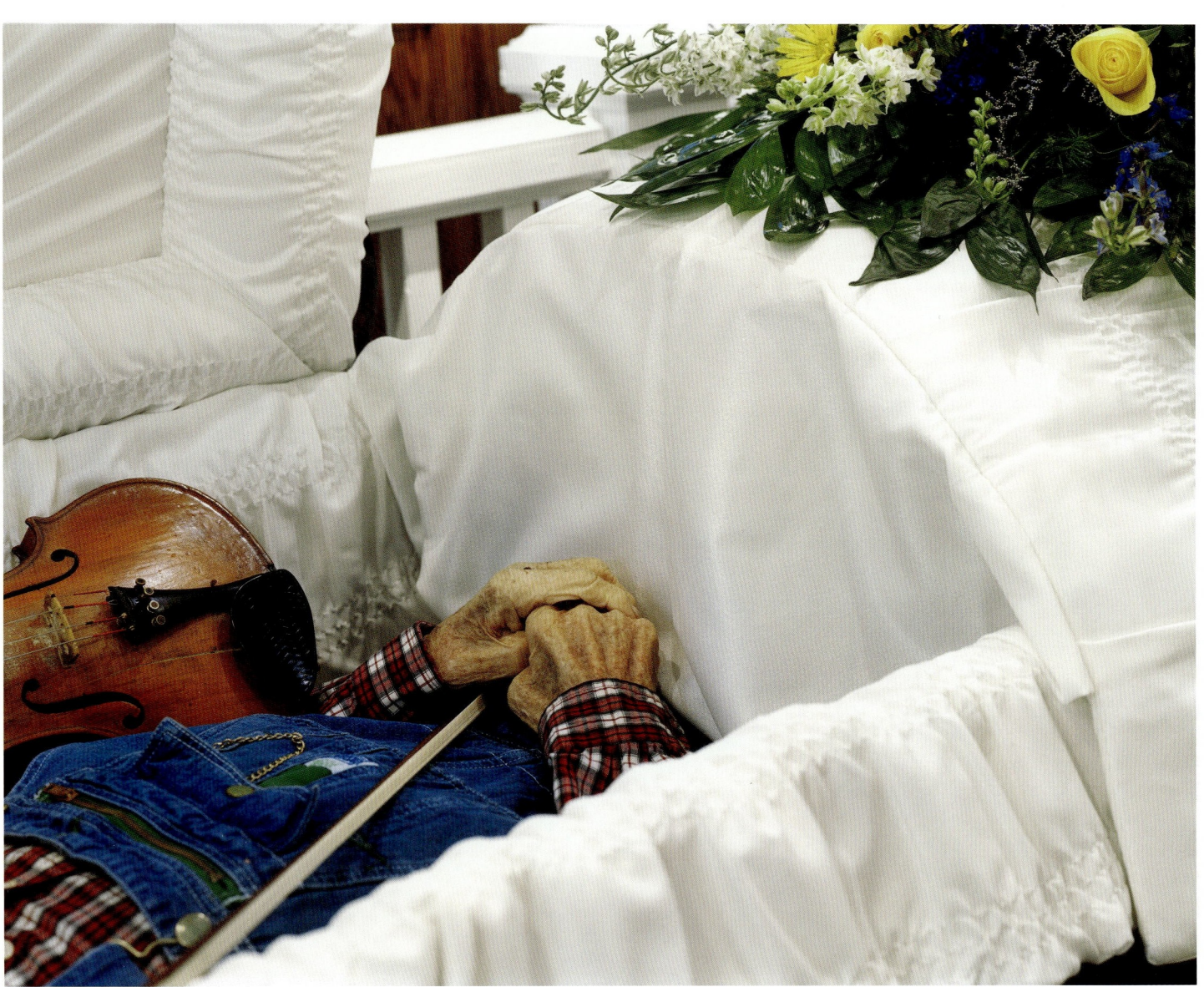

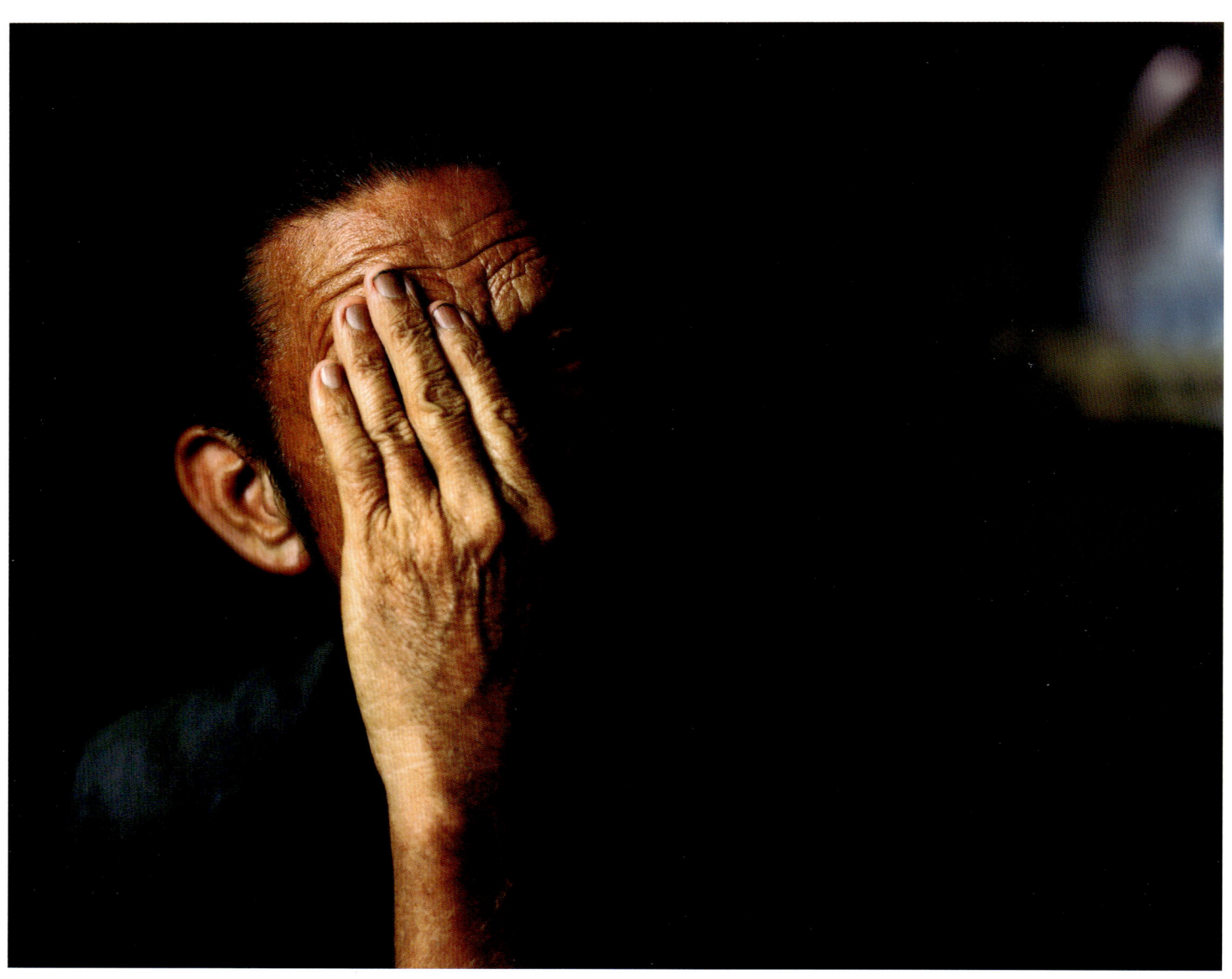

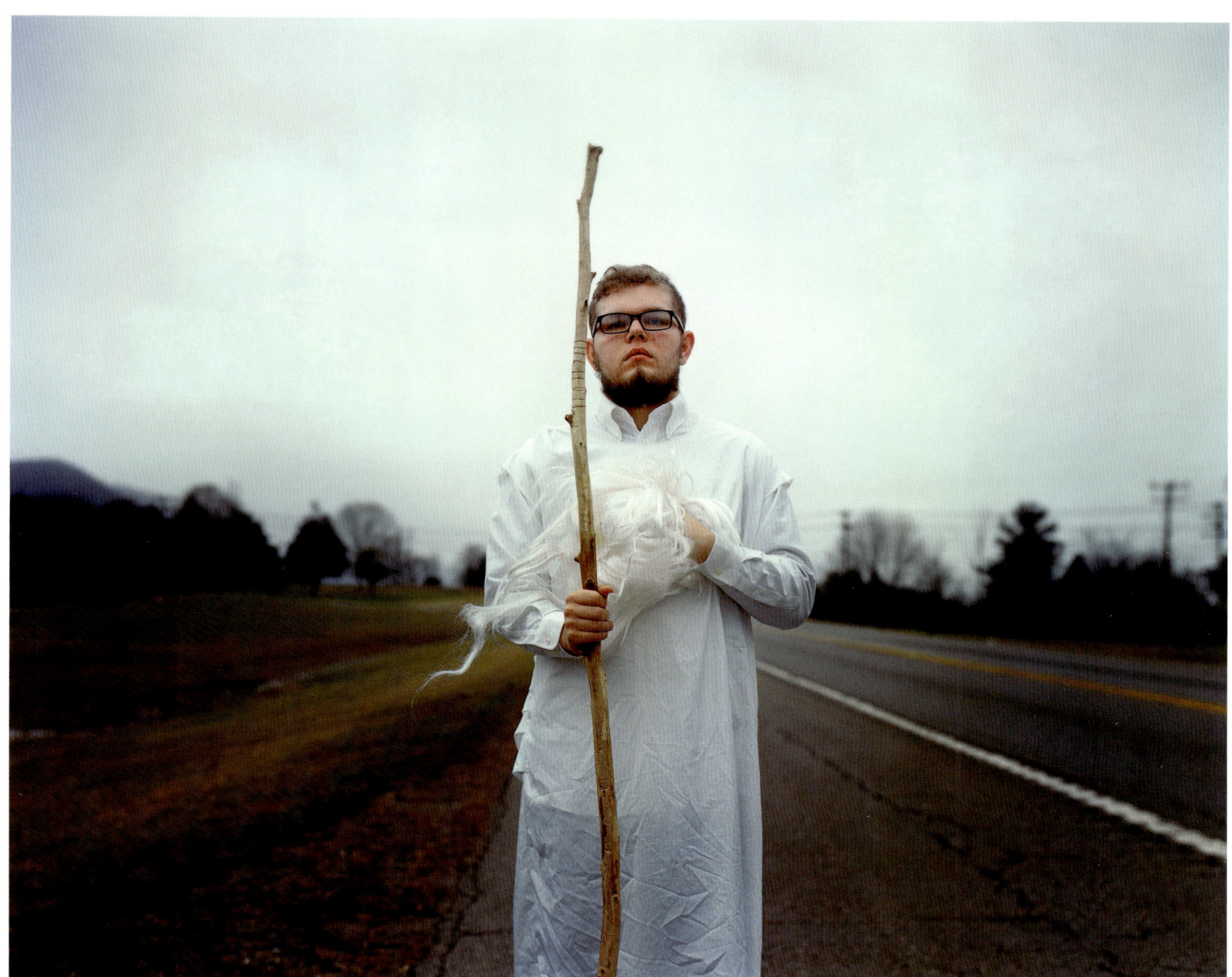

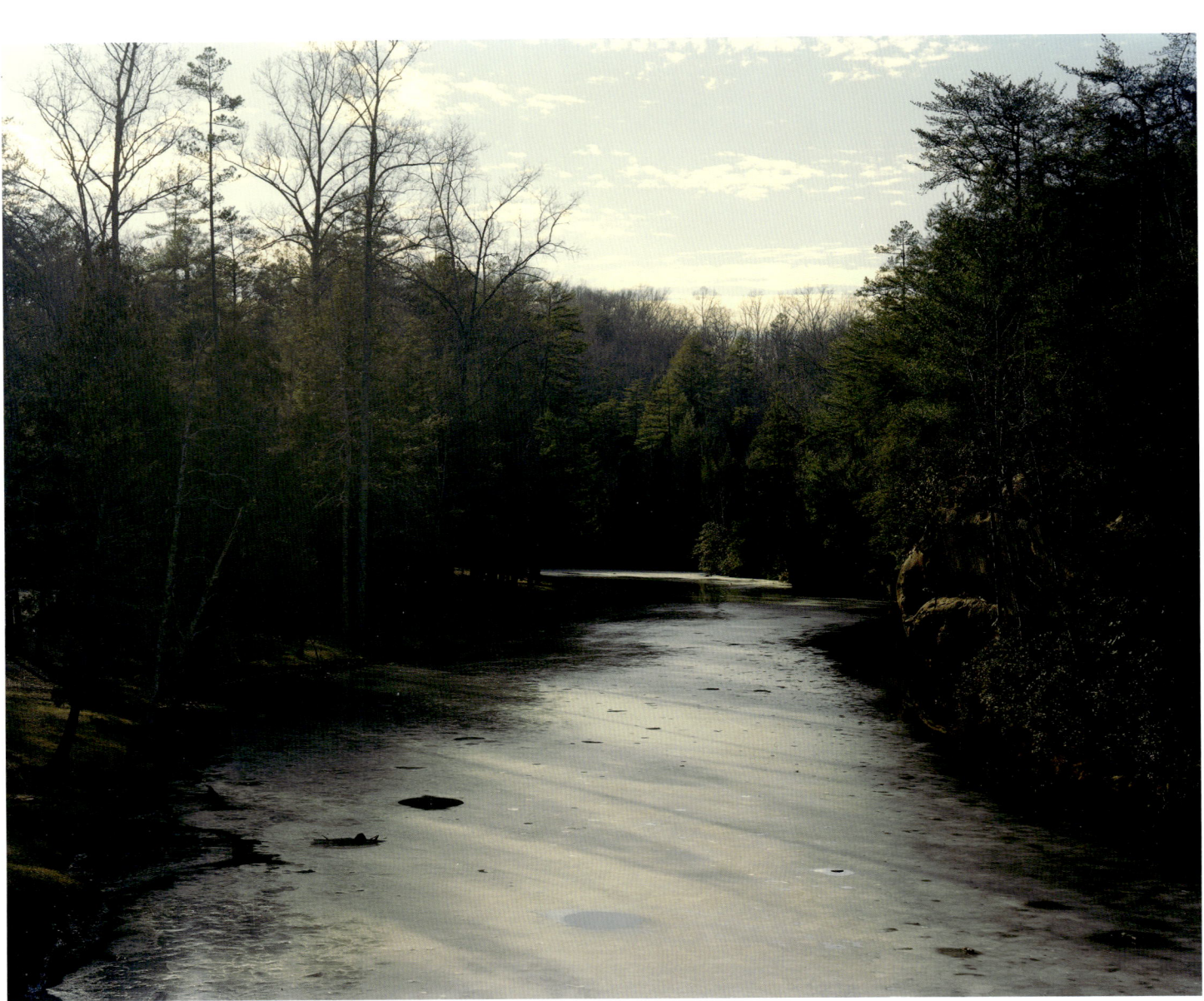

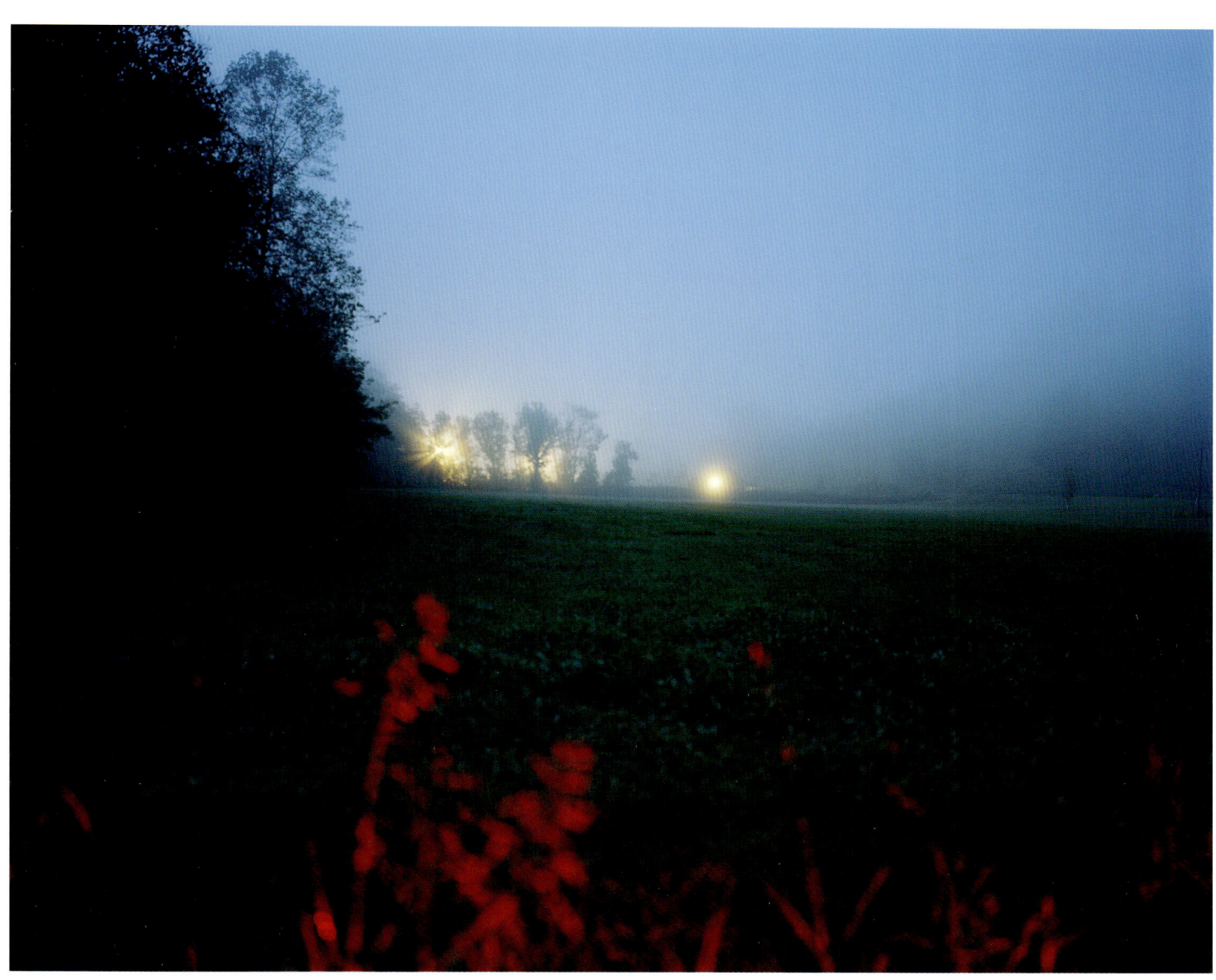

PLATES

1. A Prayer for Evelyn. Cumberland Gap, TN. 2016.

2. Evelyn's Childhood Bible. Jamestown, TN. 2016.

3. Eugene and Jobie Pray. Wilder, TN. 2017.

4. Cumberland Mountain. Crossville, TN. 2015.

5. Opal Playing Handmade Gourd Instrument. Jamestown, TN. 2017.

6. Rick and Gunsmoke the Cat. Jamestown, TN. 2017.

7. Peacock Feather. Norris, TN. 2014.

8. The Ascension. Spencer, TN. 2015.

9. Rick Forgives Kermit. Jamestown, TN. 2017.

10. Banjo-pickin' Wade Hill. Knoxville, TN. 2014.

11. Tom McCarroll's Record Player. Lenoir City, TN. 2014.

12. Ballad-singing Ema Lou Wilson. Harrogate, TN. 2014.

13. Kentucky Overlook. Pickett County, TN. 2018.

14. Charlie Higgens' Pet Cemetery. Coalmont, TN. 2014.

15. Geraldine at Arch Lake. Jamestown, TN. 2014.

16. Larry and His Handmade Zebra Dunn Gun. Jamestown, TN. 2016.

17. The Old Coon Hunter Mural at Ciderville Music Hall. Powell, TN. 2015.

18. Old Sharp Place. Jamestown, TN. 2017.

19. Charlie McCarroll at Home. Harriman, TN. 2014.

20. Evelyn Sharp and Her Old Mustang. Jamestown, TN. 2014.

21. Michael's Snakeskin. Whitleyville, TN. 2015.

22. Healing Prayer. Spencer, TN. 2015.

NATURAL RHYTHMS:
Time in the Cumberland Plateau

—Lisa Volpe

Time has a different meaning in the Cumberland Plateau. This area of east Tennessee is nestled amid the Appalachian Mountains, some of the oldest mountains in the northern hemisphere. The sensuous, gentle curves of the ancient range stand hard and resilient against the eternal sky. This landscape of soft daylight, mature green glades, and misty mornings has a particular subtlety and rhythm that is neither hurried nor lacking.

The people who inhabit this area of the world are similarly rooted in an extended concept of time. They can trace their lineage in this place back many generations. Long-held traditions are commonplace and are incorporated into daily life. While the preoccupations of the everyday are immediate and mortality is an accepted reality, prevailing religious concerns take a longer view and continually reference the eternal afterlife. Like the mountains and sky of their home, the robust and resilient lives of these Appalachian residents are sharply defined against visions of the eternal—both natural and religious.

This is not to say that there is no sense of time, but rather that time—with its emphatic presence in the landscape and lives of the Cumberland Plateau—has a different significance and worth. For outsiders, on the other hand, it seems that time has lost all meaning. Today's 24/7 culture embraces the constant connection of smartphones, the nonstop pace of the Internet, a never-ending news cycle, and an attention span that is estimated at an (ever-shrinking) eight seconds. According to art critic and essayist Johnathan Crary, even the time-delineating cycle of human sleep is now a temporal scourge to be overcome. "The scandal of sleep," he writes, "is the embeddedness in our lives of the rhythmic oscillations of solar light and darkness, activity and rest . . . that have been eradicated or neutralized elsewhere."[1] Crary suggests that our rejection of sleep is akin to a rejection of nature and its cycles. It is no wonder that Cumberland's residents, surrounded by the beauty of "rhythmic oscillations" of the sun and moon and the permanent embrace of the Appalachian Mountains, retain a reverence for time. Rachel Boillot's series *Moon Shine* is a lyrical revelation of this longevous life as it exists in this unique area.

---

[1] Johnathan Crary, 24/7: *Late Capitalism and the Ends of Sleep* (London: Verso Books, 2013): 11.

The musical tradition of the Cumberland Plateau was the catalyst for the series, but music, characterized by cadence and duration, is only a metaphor for this place. Time undoubtedly emerges as the major theme of the series and Boillot's treatment of it is both subtle and shrewd. Time, after all, is one of the governing concepts of our lives, yet we are woefully unfit to distinguish it. Our eyes may differentiate colors and shapes, our ears distinguish sounds and discover gentle cadences, and our hands feel the infinite textures of our world. Yet how does one sense time? Boillot uses the camera as an instrument to apprehend this elusive concept. In her photographs, she embraces a symbolic, sensory lexicon to evoke both eternal and mortal time. These sensory signs are heightened through Boillot's use of contrast both within single images and between different photographs in the series—soft vs. hard, gravity vs. weightlessness, music vs. silence, mortal vs. eternal. Echoing the visual contrast of the region, these binaries add complexity and underscore the significance of the work.

The photographs in *Moon Shine* are replete with tactile elements. Textures and surfaces—hard and soft, rough and smooth—are distinguishable throughout the series. While this sensory facet helps to enliven the narrative quality of the work, it also expresses the larger theme of time. In *Forrest at the Old Camaro Farm*, the hard-edged rust on the truck—a pattern of brown, gray, and white—is seen in comparison to the subject's similarly colored downy hair. Though the tactile qualities of both rust and hair are different, they are joined by the shared palette and suggest a shared source; the rust and Franklin's hair are both the product of natural time. Similarly, the sticky, delicate webs bound between the ceramic figures in *Devotional Statue* are echoed in another photograph—the soft, white waves of Geraldine's hair. Both cobwebs and hair were formed over months or years. The changes wrought by natural time are made visible in these physical elements.

Religion, with its own link to time, is denoted by other tactile elements in the photographs. Curving softly away from a rough-hewn beam, the soft peacock feather in the aptly titled *Peacock Feather* creates a textural contrast and emphasizes the symbolic nature of the plume. In the past, residents of the Cumberland Plateau raised peacocks. Though the exact reasons for this husbandry have been obscured by the intervening years, these colorful tokens remain. What is recalled, however, is their symbolic meaning. In a religious context, the peacock is a sign of the resurrection and the immortality of Christ, based on an old belief that its flesh never decayed. This religious connection is only strengthened by Boillot's placement of the feather on a wooden beam, a visual link to the cross of Christ. For the residents of the Cumberland Plateau, the peacock feather represents both their personal past and a religious eternity. In other photographs—*Cherokee Healing Prayer*, *Eugene and Jobie Pray*, and *Rick Forgives Kermit*—physical touch more directly references religion and suggests a connection between the fleeting action of a blessing and an eternal afterlife.

Coupled with a sense of touch, signs of weight or mass add further complexity to *Moon Shine*'s temporal theme. Perhaps the most overt example is *Eugene Hensley and the Jesus Rock Ministry*. The small stones this parking lot preacher dispenses are cradled heavily in his hands, their weight obvious in the taut lines of his arms. Similarly, his outfitted bus is sunk heavily into the grass behind him. Yet, in contrast to these weighty elements, half of the picture frame is filled with the open sky. This sharp contrast of weight and lightness, suggests that within a religious context the burden of earthy life is transcended in the freedom of heaven. The same message is unmistakably present in *The Ascension,* in which a heavy cinderblock is juxtaposed with a mural depicting the ascending form of Jesus. The burdens of the earth are temporary when compared to the peace of eternal heaven.

Posture—the physical weight of the body arranged in space—is equally expressive in other photographs in *Moon Shine*. In Boillot's portrait of Kathy Matthews titled *A Prayer for Evelyn*, the subject is seen from the back, her arms thrown open. Her lean frame echoes the form of the trees and branches around her, all of which reach to the sky in a posture of natural ecstasy. Her Mennonite garb, characterized by its strong contrast of dark and white, is echoed in the pattern of light and shadow on the ground. This color comparison between the pattern of light and Kathy's physical garments suggests they share an ethereal quality; there is a lightness of her soul due to her spirituality. Like the natural forms around her and her religious beliefs, Kathy is more in tune with an eternal timeframe.

Unlike Kathy, who stretches toward the heavens, other subjects in Boillot's series are captured with eyes cast down or closed, and bodies gently curved over their instruments. In *Curtis Byrge Playing at Home,*

Byrge is captured in a sublime moment. His musical labors have released his mind from his daily concerns and the silence of the photograph foregrounds that internal transcendence. Yet his body is also on display. The hard lines etched around his eyes and mouth and his age-spotted hands are frozen with the camera's capture, displayed for the viewer. Similar portraits of Charlie McCarroll, Evelyn Sharp, and others emphasize not only the religious nature of their musical devotion but also their mortal bodies. The long tradition of their music is presented in contrast to their physical decline.

Music, of course, is inevitably linked to time. Not only are songs counted out in rhythmic, temporal patterns, but music itself is a tradition. The Cumberland Plateau is filled with a diversity of songs and performances—ballads, bawdy pieces, religious numbers, instrumental tunes, and love songs—most of which have survived for generations. Yet the songs and traditions of this place are fading. Younger residents have rejected learning the music of their elders. Just as a song has a beginning and end, so do traditions and lives. Mortality is one of the natural rhythms that define the Cumberland Plateau. Boillot's photographs do not shy away from this truth. Tom McCarroll, who is photographed with his instruments, is later pictured in his casket, his fiddle still near his hands. Similarly, Evelyn Sharp, seen both in her home with her guitar and outside gazing to the sky, passed away since the creation of those photographs.

Time has a different meaning in photography. Photo theorists from Siegfried Kracauer to Roland Barthes to Susan Sontag have explored the inherent relationship between photography and time. Of all the artistic media, it is perhaps best equipped to express time, presenting as it does a lasting image of a moment that has passed—the "that-has-been," as Barthes called it. As this constructed term suggests, photography unites the past and present, sustaining it for the future. Boillot's artistic project, *Moon Shine*, utilizes the atemporal nature of the photograph to create a sensitive study of the Cumberland Plateau—a region in which matters of time are similarly deep-rooted. Boillot produces images ripe with sensory elements that reference the eternal forces of both nature and the religious afterlife, and confront the ultimate reality of mortal death. In the moonlit shadow of an ancient mountain range, time is measured by different metrics. *Moon Shine* celebrates this difference, safeguarding a past for the present and future.

AUTHOR'S NOTE

—Rachel Boillot

I first went to Tennessee in June of 2014. My intention was to spend two months making photographs for a park ranger. The subject matter was opaque to me, but I needed a gig.

Folklorist, naturalist, and musician Bob Fulcher, who currently manages Tennessee's Cumberland Trail State Scenic Park, was initially dismayed by my lack of knowledge regarding old-time country music. Turned out this was to be the focus of the job. Bob believes that preserving cultural resources is just as important as land conservation in this region, which is the more explicit prerogative of the parks system. But in Tennessee, music is "in the water," as the saying goes.

I had absolutely no knowledge of country music—not to mention its history and the old-time traditions that preceded contemporary country music.

What I learned was that there was a time when families played together at home for the sheer revelry of sounding out in celebration after a hard day's work. They played thankfully for another day gone by. There was genuine soul in that. It was not a commercial endeavor; it was expression. On that first day, Bob and I spent hours being chauffeured in a state SUV while he brought me up to speed. The next day, he had a park emergency—a child lost in the woods. He shot me a hasty email with a list of names and numbers. The subject line read "Get Busy." So I made some phone calls and started making pictures.

I met the McCarrolls first. Tom McCarroll was eighty-six years old at the time. We lost him on September 4, 2015. Tom collected pocket watches, and I gave him one on his eighty-seventh birthday. I always felt like this was a kinship between us. What else does a photographer do but gather time?

Tom's younger brother Charlie was not well when I met him. When I reported this to his friends and family, all were dubious. They assumed I was naive to the hard-living lifestyle of a mountain man.

Truth be told, I certainly was. I was raised in New York's well-to-do Westchester County. But I knew that Charlie was very sick. I started visiting daily to check in on him, even though I wasn't taking pictures. One day I found him on his deathbed. I was unsure whether I should intervene. He wanted to die, and I wasn't sure what quality of life would remain for him if he did survive. I'm absolutely thrilled to report that he has

since adjusted well to life in the nursing home, where he plays the fiddle regularly in the cafeteria and has two different girlfriends in opposite wings of the home, where he can wheel himself surreptitiously without the other knowing.

I met Opal and Evelyn, the Sharp sisters, soon thereafter. When I first called Evelyn, she couldn't hear me. She thoroughly cursed out the purported telemarketer calling her. She demanded: "Is this Trump calling?" She banged down the phone after her final words: "You bastard." She later explained to me that she couldn't hear high, fine voices over the phone, especially not ones that spoke in a Yankee tongue.

When I called her sister Opal that first day, I asked her if she could meet me at Evelyn's so I could photograph them together. With great surprise, she responded that she was over ninety years old and couldn't drive. It was then that I started to realize this was a different sort of project than I had embarked upon before.

After two months, I left. It was the end of the contract. I had another commission in North Carolina and a teaching job at Duke University. I was moving into my newly rented apartment when Bob unexpectedly called me in the blue of December. I was expecting it to be my mother, who had come to assist with the move. I answered immediately.

"Rachel, I'm in a bit of pickle," he said. "I need an audio engineer for the record label." I replied, "Bobby, I'm no audio engineer, but I'd come back in a heartbeat." The phone cut out at that moment, and Bob was gone.

Two days later, Bob returned the call. "Did you say you'd do it in a heartbeat?"

I soon found myself running a record label for a park ranger. I was a still photographer ill-equipped for the task, but excited to spend more time with the people I had met that first summer.

Housing was provided as part of my contract. Technically, I was an AmeriCorps service member. I stayed in a double-wide trailer before relocating to the head of the Sequatchie Valley, where a rather enormous cave loomed in my backyard. I finally landed in an old FEMA trailer from Hurricane Katrina, which the Park Service had kindly migrated my way. I spent the next several months camping in Cove Lake State Park without heat or running water.

So I showered at Evelyn's house and gradually moved in with an extremely cranky ninety-five-year-old woman. Cranky to the extent that she would change the spelling of her name daily just so that she could chastise those of yesterday. "That's not my name. You got it wrong," she'd say. "That's not my name anymore." One day she was "Evelyn," "Evelene" the next.

Evie continued to be hot and bothered by Trump's candidacy for the American presidency. "I just don't understand, Rachel," she'd say. "It's like he's paying his way in. Bastard. And why does he hate Mexicans? They's good people and hard workers. What would we do without them? Deporting 'em? Bastard. That'd be like losing half the country. Our entire workforce. Does Trump want to do what they do? Phew."

Evie lived in Jamestown, Tennessee, one of the main hubs along the annual Highway 127 Yard Sale: the longest yard sale in the world. I met Eugene Hensley on the 127 bypass during the 2014 event. I photographed him on that day holding stones in his hand. Years later, Eugene has become a dear friend. He is a mostly beloved local character on the Jamestown scene, where he holds court in the Walmart parking lot the first weekend of every month, scurrying about to distribute his Jesus Rocks flanked by Jobie the parrot. Gene does not believe in denomination; he simply believes that all should feel the love of Christ. I'm happy to report that Jobie was recently wedded to a second parrot named Toby.

Not too long ago, I had to bail Gene out of jail. As a recovering alcoholic and addict, his congregation is largely comprised of locals recovering from opioid addiction in a region where these pills are highly overprescribed. Recently, Gene has been suffering from kidney stones. The country doctor recommended he drink some beer to help him pass the stones. So Gene went on a bender and downed a six-pack in approximately ten minutes while filling up his water jugs at the local spring. He then collided with his neighbor's truck head-on trying to make it back home. A bad situation worsened when the neighbor angrily stormed out of his vehicle, brandishing a pistol he declared to be loaded, while wildly waving it above his head. The drunken Eugene panicked, got back in his school bus, and high-tailed it home—where the local deputy awaited him, of course, with everybody knowing everybody in the hollow of Wilder, Tennessee. He was imprisoned for a drunken hit-and-run and had his license revoked. After his release from jail, Gene is back on the road again, sober, and helping opioid addicts recover—albeit in his own unique fashion—in a place where the epidemic is rampant.

In 2015, I recorded Opal Sharp Wright singing the rare ballad "Zebra Dunn" while rocking in her chair at home. Bobby and I later released the recording on "Sharp's Hornpipe II: The Sharp Family Recordings." Several months later, Opal's son Larry wanted to show me something. I assumed it was evidence of a recent bear attack that had left permanent damage to the walls of their double-wide trailer. Instead, Larry presented me with the Zebra Dunn gun, hand-made out of a two-by-four he'd found in the yard and painted with zebra stripes and cheetah print in commemoration of the recording. It was made to be my height exactly: 4'10-1/2". I've let Larry hang on to the gun; he has far more use for it than I—but not before I made a picture.

Larry routinely finds discarded objects and repurposes them to create his artwork. The same year I met Eugene Hensley at the Highway 127 Sale, Larry found an old gourd that no one wanted. He threw it in the backseat, took it home, and made it into an instrument that his mother could play. That's another picture and another story.

I met the legally blind ballad singer Curtis Byrge when the *Knoxville News Sentinel* did a story on my work. Curtis has never been able to drive due to poor eyesight, but he walks many miles to play his music. The *Knoxville News Sentinel* featured me and Curtis on the front page. A few months later, I got word that Curtis had written a song about the event and had been playing it at the Oak Ridge flea market, where he walks every Saturday morning to perform. The lyrics go, "Rachel, you're an angel with a camera, just makin' a legend out of me." Initially, I was just horribly embarrassed by the song. I've never wanted to insert myself into my work, even if it is my work, always framed by my own personal perspective. But I've made my peace with the song now. My photographs made Curtis proud of himself, and I couldn't ask for more.

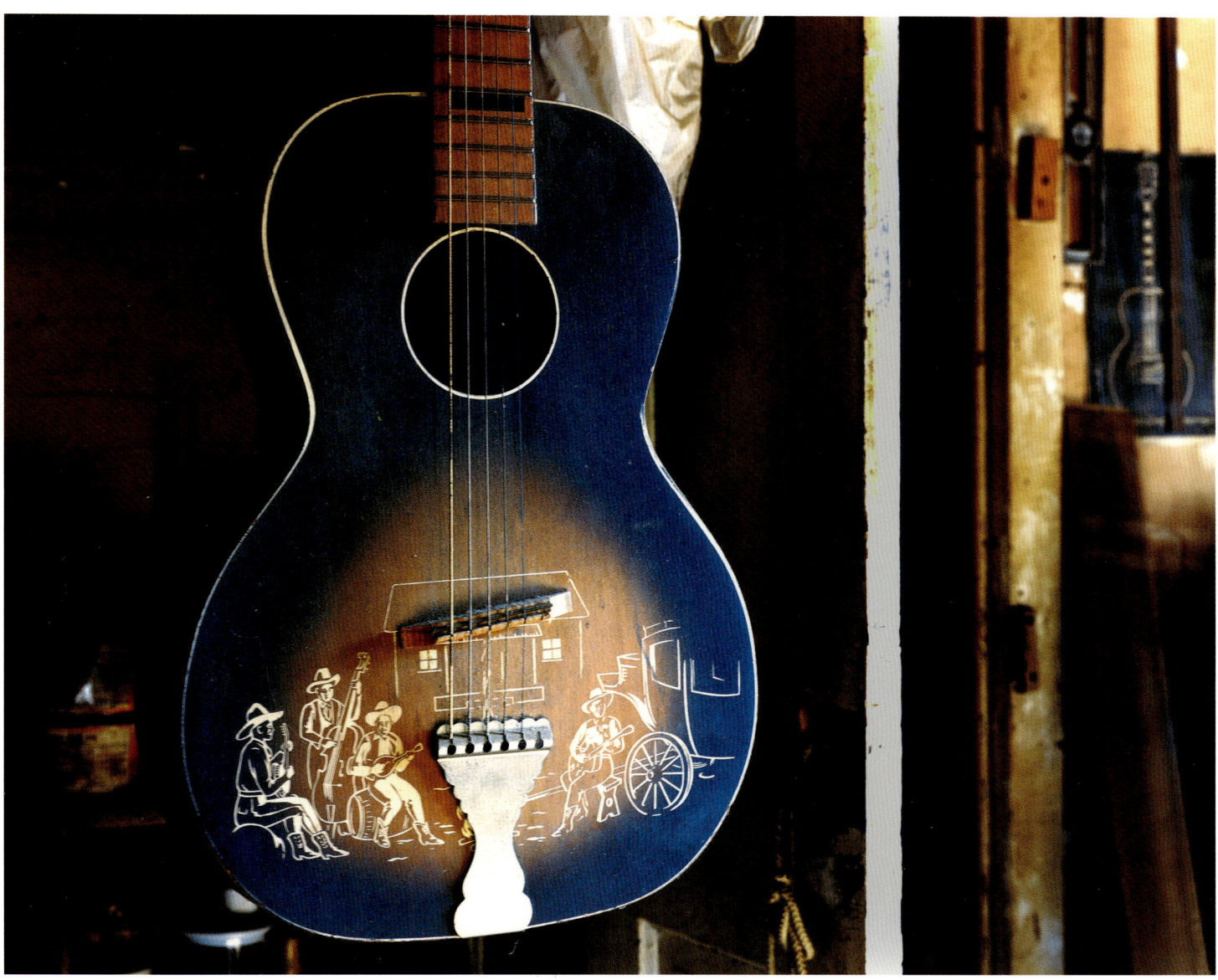

IN THEIR OWN WORDS

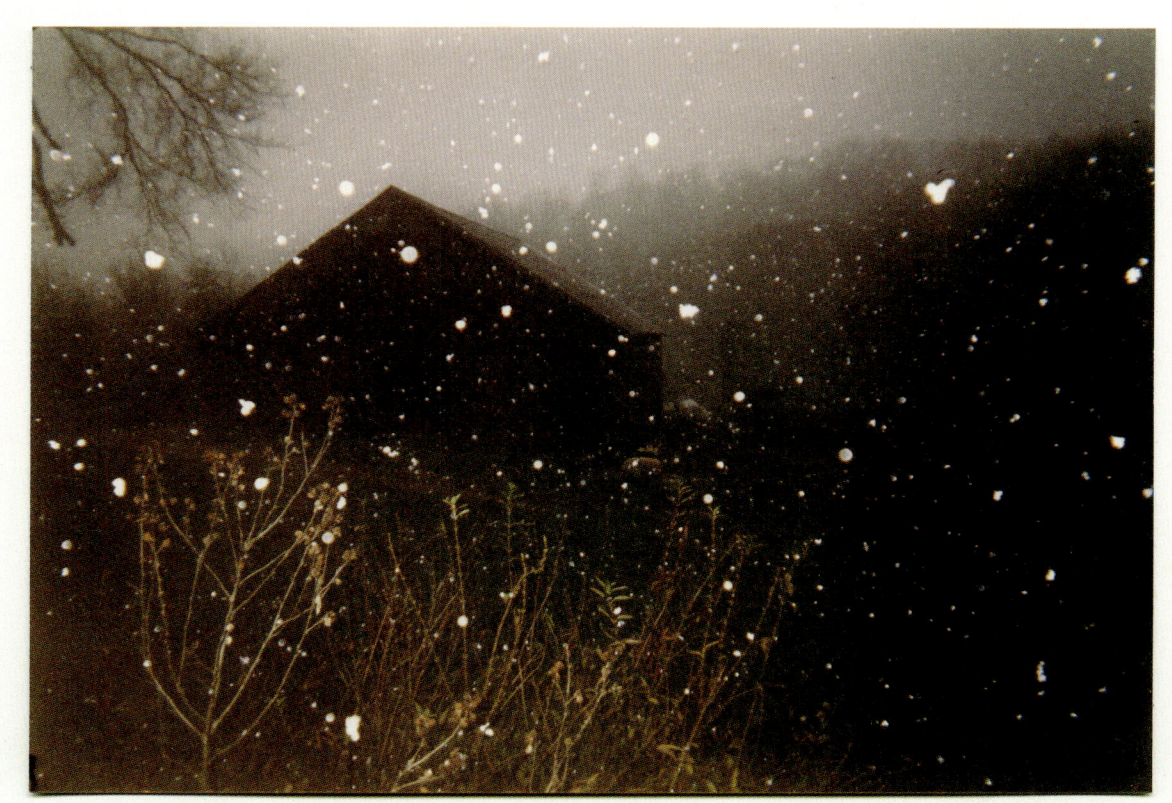

Conatser Hollow, ca. 2003

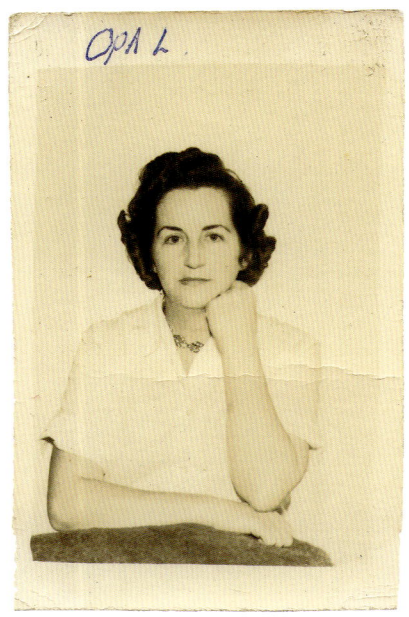

Opal Sharp Wright
around age 35

OPAL SHARP WRIGHT

I was born in the roaring twenties. My dad was playing music up a storm at that time, going to dances and playing his fiddle for 'em. He'd pick the banjo for us kids and we'd dance.

My daddy, he was a moonshiner. I'm not ashamed of it cause the camp had moved away and left us over there and wasn't no job or nothing. And you know, he was crippled, he couldn't work no regular job. I guess dad had to feed his kids. He had three brothers that lived over there by him and they'd help him sometime, they'd all gather up there at the still and you could hear 'em a-singing and making music. He made it in places where he thought the law wouldn't get him. He made it under a rockhouse. And when he got it made, me and my sister Evelyn, we went with him down under there. And we would carry it on into the house. Carried two and a half gallons a piece.

They'd have a midnight supper every Saturday night. Stay up all night play music after they ate at midnight. Dad's friends, they lived in Monticello, Kentucky, and they'd get on them big black horses and have cowboy hats on and have them guitars tied on to them horses and we could hear 'em coming a mile or two away up that rocky road, you know, just running them old horses and hollerin'. They'd play music all night long. All night.

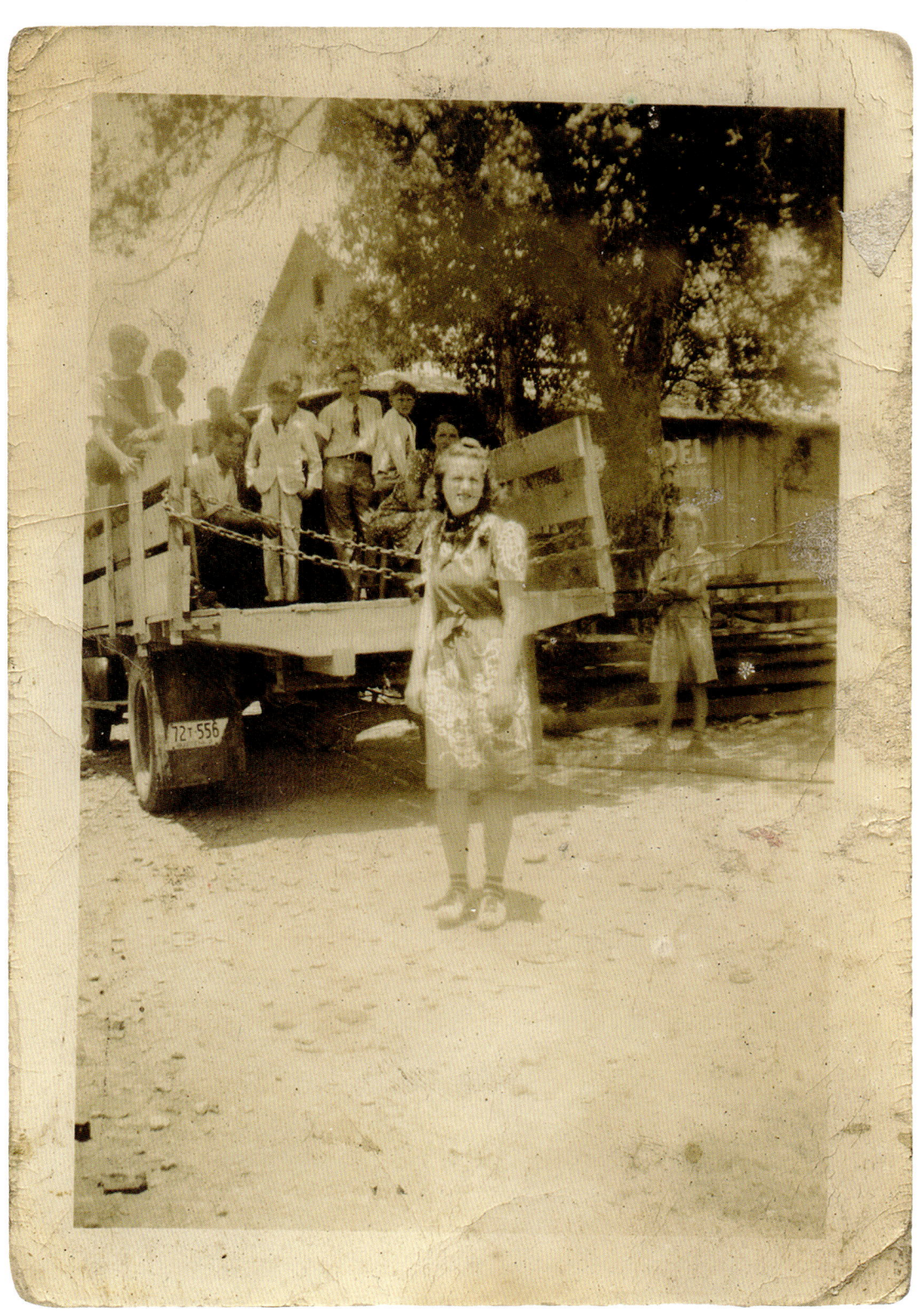

Opal Sharp Wright at the homecoming celebration in Boatland, TN, when she was 17 years old, 1940

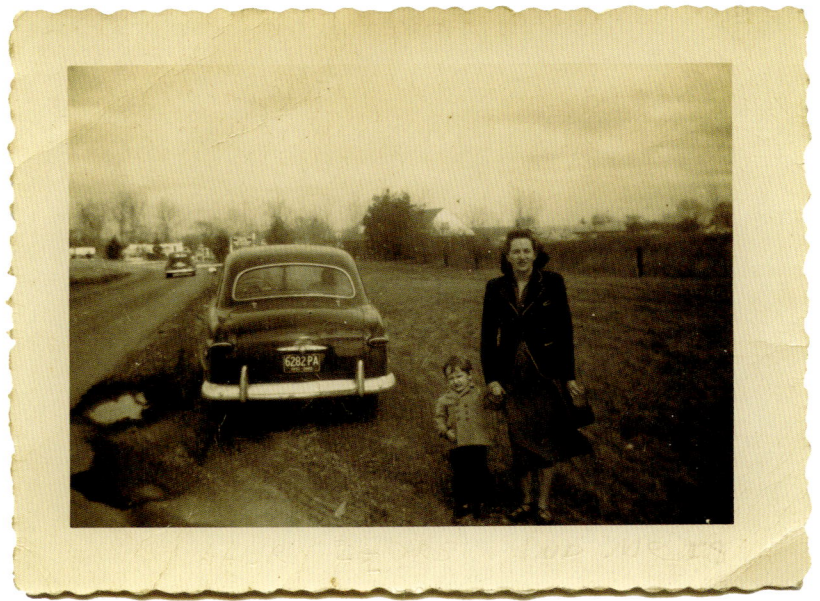

Opal Sharp Wright and her son Larry on Rural Route 5 in Muncie, IN, 1952

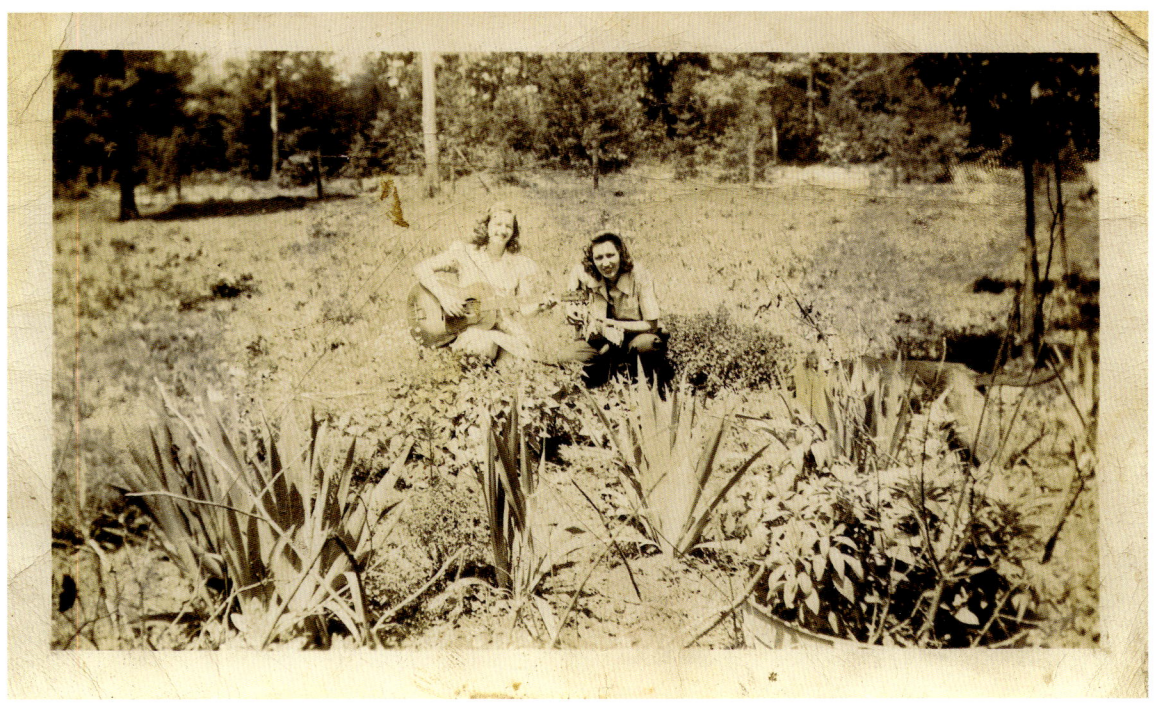

Opal Sharp Wright and Evelyn at the Old Squirrel Upchurch place in Rock Creek, TN, ca. 1939

Me and my sister Evelyn, we used to play together. We started when we was about twelve and fourteen year old. I'd sing and she'd play the guitar. We'd go to churches and play music and they'd send for us, they called us the Sharp Sisters. They'd have to come and get us and bring us back home, that's the only way we had. Didn't have no car, no nothin'. Back when Mom and Dad was first married, why, they even had to ride a buggy. A one-horse buggy. Can you imagine that?

Sure enough, I growed up playing music. And I got married in 1940. Well, in 1941, you know, the war got started. December 7. President Roosevelt declared war on the Japanese empire. My husband, he come in from work and said, "We've got a war. We've got a war started." Said, "We got to leave here. We've got to go and help." Course, up North, every factory was makin' defense plant stuff. Muncie [Indiana] was a boomtown. We heared about it, and just like the Clampetts we went to Muncie! We went up there and got jobs in defense plants. At General Motors they gave me a riveting job. I put rivets, you know, in airplane wings 'cause I was just right for the wing. I was a good hand. Yeah, I guess I was just like Rosie the Riveter.

After the war was over, I decided it was time for me to go home. I missed seeing the pretty trees turnin' yellow and red down here. Lawd, I'd get so homesick! I just about died I'd get so homesick. I'd even write and tell Mom and Dad to send me some colored leaves.

So I moved back down here. Come back down here and bought this place and raised my kids up right here. And I still played my music. Still today, sometimes I'll get out on the porch—I just get in there and pick what I'm gonna play and me and ol' Daisy, we just cut loose.

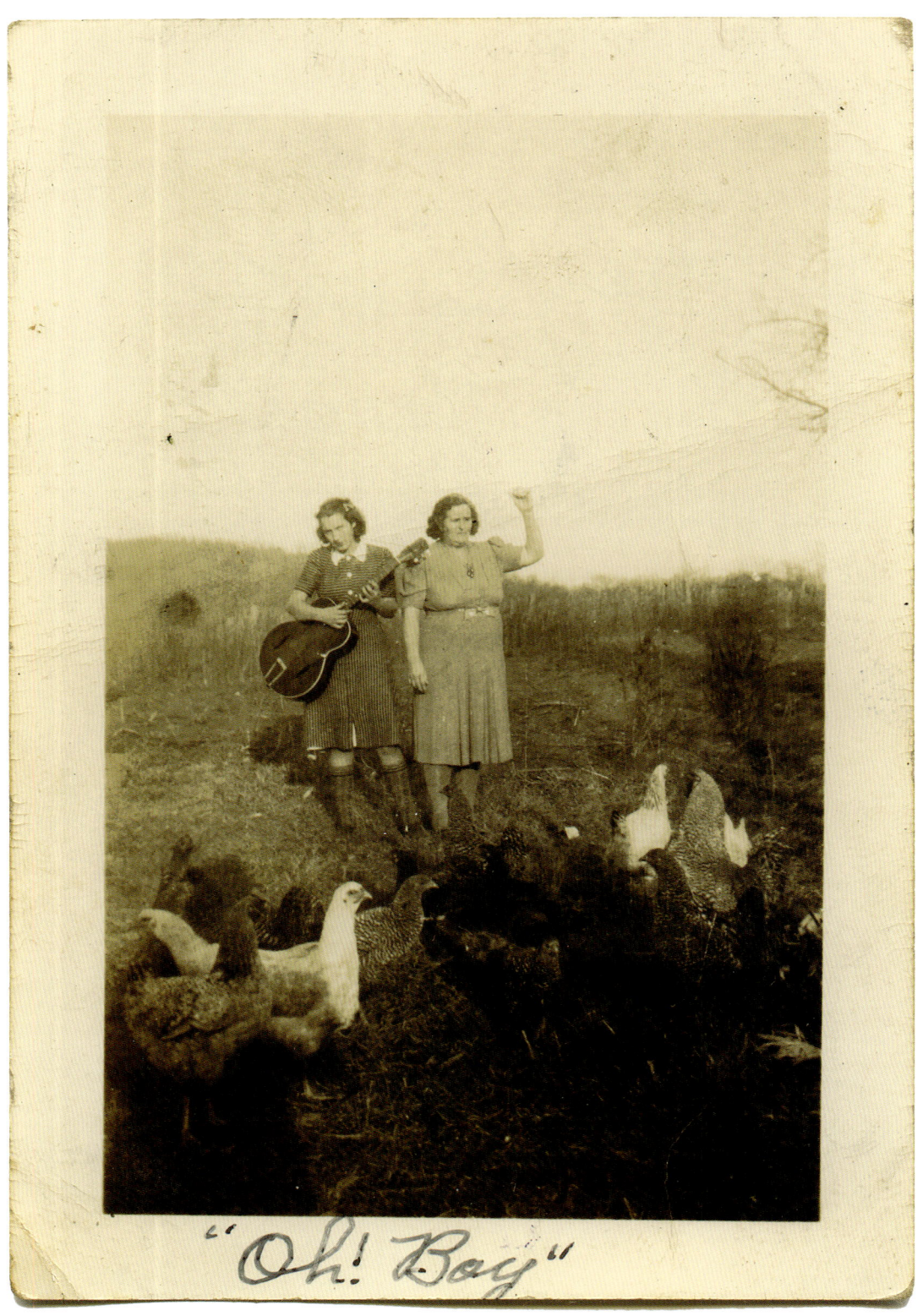

"Oh! Boy"

Evelyn Sharp Conatser and her Aunt Dolly in Pall Mall, TN, ca. 1937

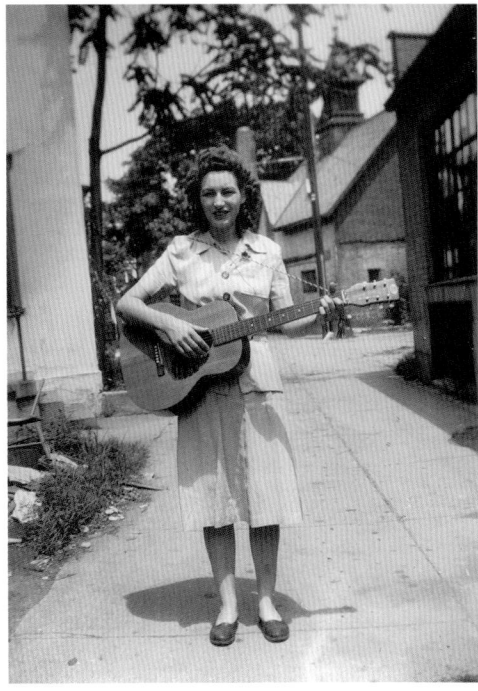

Evelyn Sharp Conatser in Dayton, OH, ca. 1942

EVELYN SHARP CONATSER

We lived on the dish of a mountain. We had no radio, no TV, no telephone, just the farm. I plowed the mule, I hoed corn, worked in the garden, all kinds of stuff. Growed everything we eat. All my life I worked. Since I was eight year old. And I was the meanest kid you ever seen in your life. They couldn't make 'em any meaner today.

Dad made some whisky. Made some money off of it. Wasn't nothin' to make moonshine back then! Big shots in Monticello'd come for it. Gave us more for it.

That was the only kind of music we had, what we played. That was what we done in those days. Back then there wasn't no commodities, there wasn't no handouts . . . wasn't no Social Security, wasn't no nothin'. Was rough. Was money then, we didn't know anything about it.

I was just five year old and I sat in the room, Dad didn't say a word, and I was a-watchin' every chord he made on the guitar. But he wouldn't let me touch it. They all got down with the flu, the old killing kind back then. Everybody was in the bed but me. I was the only one didn't take it. And I thought, "I know how to play that guitar, can't none of them stop me now, I'll just go there and play." I got up and climbed up to get that

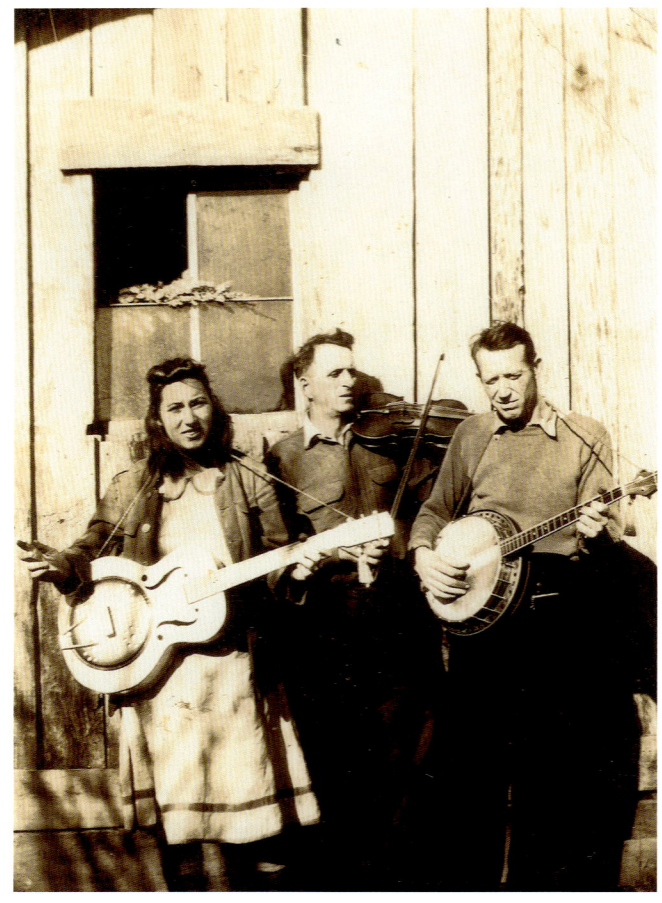

Evelyn Sharp Conatser, Wright Morris, and John Sharp, ca. 1935

old guitar. I got up on Dad's bed, sat at the foot of it and started playin' "Old Sally Goodin," and singing it, too, and boy, from then on, he made me play!

We used to play music at town here. And I played till I thought to my soul I was gonna die. And I quit, I was about to go to sleep. And Dad pecked me on the head with the fiddle bow, wakin' me up!

It was for people like old Donald Trump. Just it was all Democrats then. That's who we played for. They'd have their big meetings, and we'd do the music.

I was married on the 23rd day of December. We got married and me and him used to go squirrel huntin'. Killed twenty one day. First time I ever shot my shotgun I killed a squirrel.

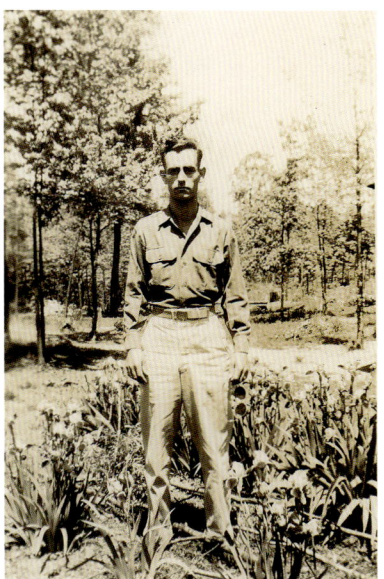

*Kermit Conatser,
ca. 1940*

I married the wrong man when I met him. Kermit was a preacher's boy. Could get by with anything.

This was the worst thing he done to me in all my lifetime.

I was a playin' music down at the park. And he come down there with a loaded pistol and stuck it in my back. He said, "I'm gonna kill you. And you're gonna go, if you don't I'm gonna shoot this place up right here. I've got a shotgun in the car and I've got a pistol." And I got in the car with him, afraid he'd hurt somebody down there.

He took me a way down in the woods. There's a big pine tree standing up over there. He said, "Get out and stand in front of that pine tree." Said, "I'm gonna kill you." I said, "Alright. I'm ready to go." I got out and stood in front of that pine tree, stretched out my arms like that and I said, "Now whatever you do, don't miss me." And when I said that, he dropped that gun. He said, "You wanting to die that bad, I'll just let you live and aggravate you to death."

I had a nervous breakdown just shortly after he tried to kill me. I was trying to get over it. I talked to a bishop of the church. He asked me if there was anything in my life that I liked to do. I said, "Yeah. I used to like to play music back then." He said, "Go do it again."

Oh, I decided, I'll put me on my cowboy hat, and I'll put me patent blue jeans on and I'll go down there and see what's going on. Down at the park. I heared that fiddle a-playin. And the banjo. So I borrowed me an old piece of a guitar. I didn't have no guitar, my sister-in-law had broke it over Bill Stevens' head. And I finally got that one there. And playing music again—that saved my whole life. It's the truth. Playing music saved my whole life.

RICK CONATSER

(Evelyn's son)

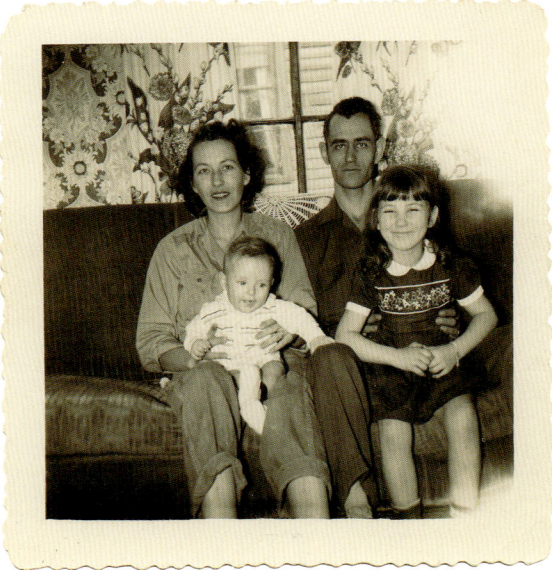

Evelyn Sharp Conatser holding Rick Conatser (left) and Kermit Conatser holding Hope Conatser (right) in Jamestown, TN, ca. 1953

Course, they was raised with nothing. So, they made their music and they enjoyed it. It was rough in the Depression. It was really rough. And the music would make you dance. It just seems like everytime everybody got together is was musical, always.

Mom, she'd sang to us when we was kids, you know. Ah, just old-timey songs. I don't remember the names.

We didn't look at it like it was anything special, the music. It was just part of the family. It was just what they done. But it wasn't sad—it was uplifting and joyful. I mean, you wanted to dance. And then, if you got to looking around a little, there was a few of 'em nipping a few in there with that old stuff they made, but they had a good time with it.

The Sharps, they was all Democrats. They'd fight you over it. If you was a Republican, they didn't want much to do with you. They always said the Democrats was for the poor man, you know. They thought that the Democrats was gonna help 'em.

But I'm proud to be a part of the family, I sure am. They—I growed up in a good place around here. It's beautiful. I even went off one time to make my fortune up North, you know, and I stayed a week. After one week, I found a job. I told the fella, said, "I want to work—just long enough to get enough money to get back home." And he worked me a week. And he tried to get me to stay, he said, "I like your work, I'll get you a place where you can stay here if you'll stay," and I said, "Nope. I'm goin' home." And I come back and I been here ever since.

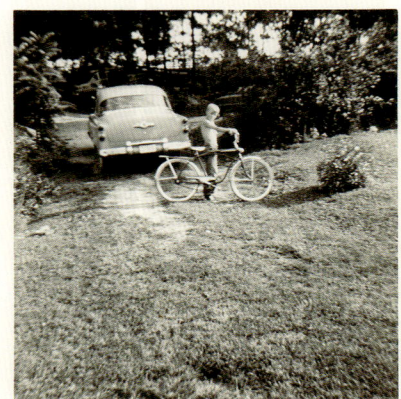

Rick Conatser, Jamestown, TN, ca. 1958

I sure growed up in a good place around here. It's beautiful. These mountains . . . it's just like being home. All this land. I'm home here.

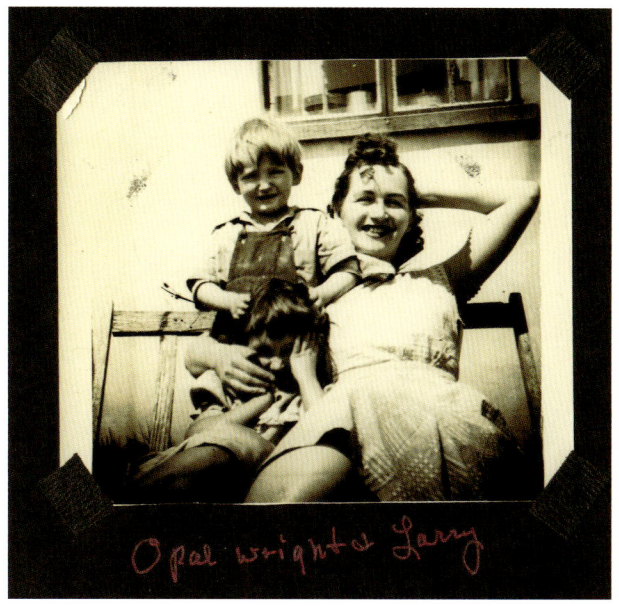

Larry and Opal Sharp Wright, ca. 1952

LARRY WRIGHT (Opal's son)

I started ridin' the mule when I was twelve year old. We had a mule, and I was in charge of it. Old Rube. We always had a mule, cause we was loggers, me and Daddy was. Never did finish school, I had to work. We always got the high spots. We had to go down under the mountain and walk back over top of it through the woods cuttin' timber.

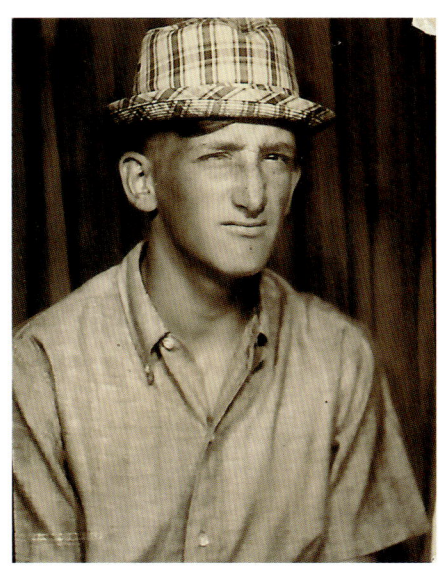

Larry Wright in Jamestown, TN, ca. 1965

Except they closed it off now. Everything is owned by the government now. Who is the government anyhow?

We got an idiot for president. As far as I'm concerned, we don't have a president anymore. When Obama left, we ain't got none. We got a paper doll up there. He don't know how to do nothing. He might know how to get rich, but I could run a government better than he does. Trump put on a red cap and he got the mountain man's vote. He promised a bunch of stuff he don't know anything about. It's a farce. It's a big joke on the United States.

FORREST FRANKLIN (Evelyn's grandson)

There was so much gunplay when I was a kid . . . there was holes in the wall. Made me kindly grow up not to like guns too good. Course, still at that time I thought that was normal stuff. That was just a normal way of life for me, gunplay was. I didn't think nothing of it. S'like when that uh, one girl, back when I was in kindergarten, brought a gun to school to shoot a girl she was upset at, and—and she come in the gym she pulled her out, out of her backpack and it went off and shot another girl through the arm. I never thought anything of it, you know. Just another gun going off.

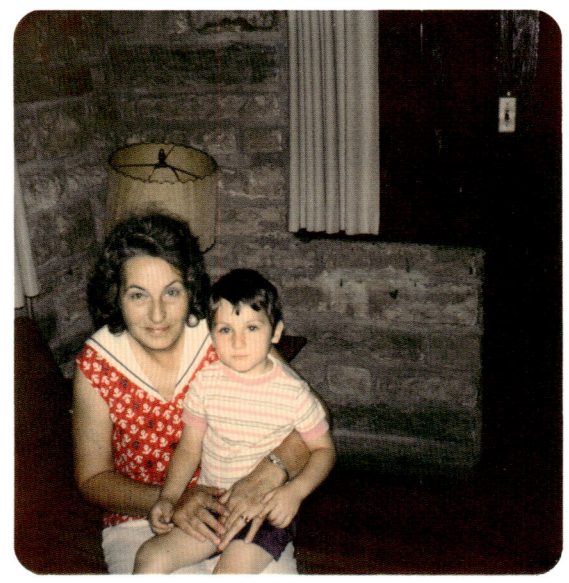

Forrest and Evelyn Sharp Conatser in Jamestown, TN, ca. 1976

Everybody was freaking out all around me, wantin' everybody to lay down. I said, "What in the world?" And they was screaming at me to lay down, get on the floor. I said "Why? It's just a gun going off." Made me lay down anyway and I felt like a fool. What in the world were we laying down for? Cause someone was shootin'?

That old music originated from Ireland, you know, and it's come into here. I mean, I was raised in it, so it's with me. Been with me all my life. And sometimes I can think back on them tunes and play 'em off in my head or something. And it'll take me back.

I think, "When they're all dead, I may be the only one left that has it." Then it's gone. When I'm gone. The songs that I know . . .

I really appreciated having them. Cause I knowed that if time lasted long enough and nothing happened to us, lived long enough for the future to come, you know, I knowed that was all gonna be well in to the past. I think it kinda makes me feel like I'd like to be able to find a little place that I can put my foot in time and just kindly pull myself back in there and enjoy it again, you know, just for a little while.

I really shouldn't think it like this, but I think, "I wished I could talk to this person or spent more time with this person question." Ask this person some more questions. You know, talk about old time mountain music and stuff. Mostly what I'm seeing right now is a bunch of past. Thinkin' about the past and that's basically what I'm seeing right now is a lot of past.

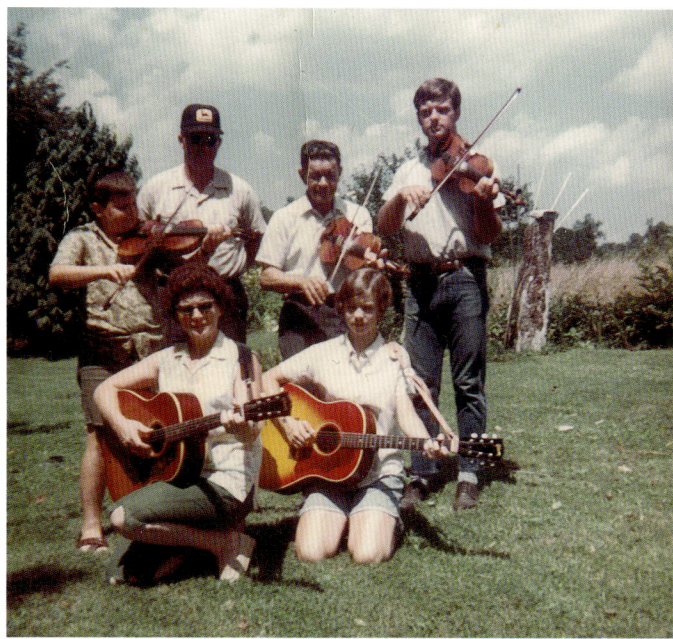

Ema Lou Wilson and friends, year unknown

EMA LOU WILSON

Granny would sing all the time when I was growing up. Oh yeah, she'd just sing all the time around the house, fixing supper. Hymns, you know. Ones like "Just Over Jordan." I can just see Granny going about, cooking her dinner and singing all those old songs. She sang all the time. I have a book at home where I wrote down a lot of these old songs. 'Cause I didn't want them to be destroyed.

Like the ones my Granny used to sing.

People don't sing like they used to. It's a shame for all those old songs to be gone. Honey, it's a shame! But the modern generation would never care about that. I guess is one reason it's disappearing. They don't seem to have the time for it.

I can't sing anymore now, honey. Always just a song, I guess. But I really had fun with my music. There'll never be more music like that. Yeah, them old times. Them's all passed. Always just a song, I guess.

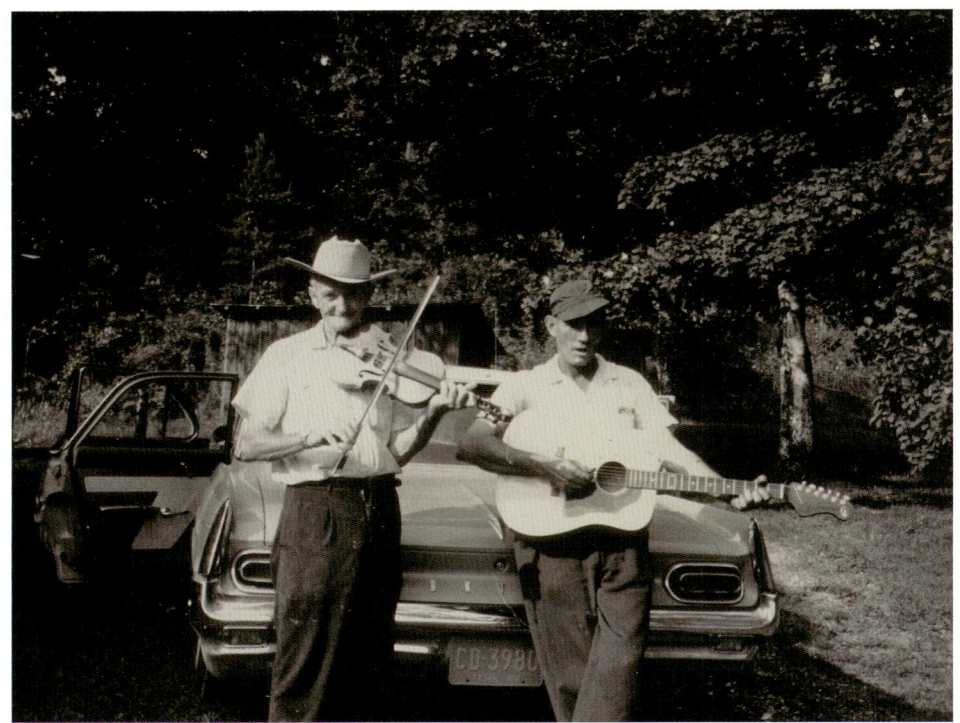

Tom McCarroll and his father Jimmy McCarroll in Lenoir City, TN, ca. 1965

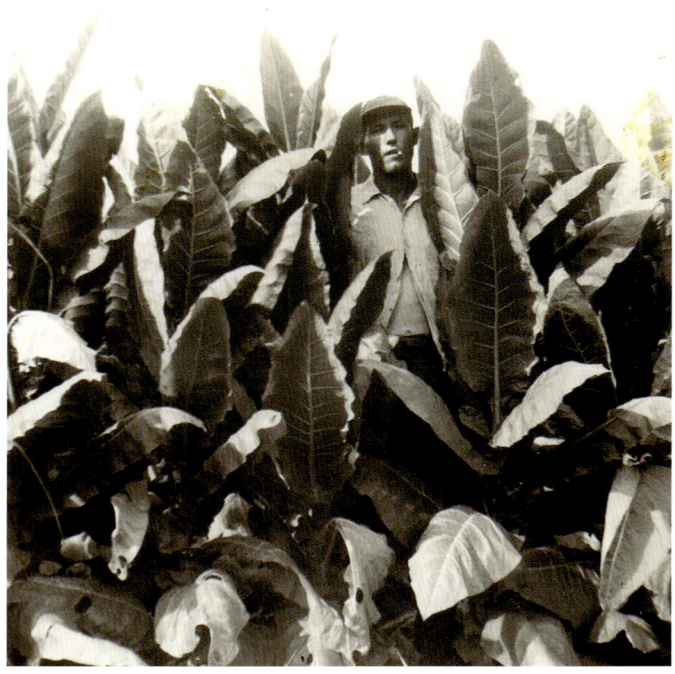

Tom McCarroll, ca. 1938

TOM McCARROLL

In the Depression, it was hand-to-mouth, that all! Shoo. We didn't worry about what we had, because everyone else was just like us, they didn't have nothing either.

Daddy worked on the farm, and he worked the coal mines off and on. Yeah, we used to move so much from one coal mine to another, we had an old rooster and if a truck pulled up in the yard he'd sit down and cross his legs.

Course, Daddy's been all over the world playing music, too. He was a showman. Never had a car, but he'd just hoof it on!

Me, I grew up playing music and working. Always worked. I was farming tobacco before we moved to town here. Got me a job and started building this house. Years ago, that way. Yep, built this here house by myself. Brick by brick. And this house has got 28,000 bricks in it. Worked a job in town by day, came home and laid brick by night. Just built it up around us. Got the basement fixed first, so we moved in there, and I just kept building on up. We lived down in there till I got the rest of the house done. Two years, all told. I guess it was two years. But when we got it done, we didn't owe nobody a dime on it.

Lived here with my wife Polly till she died. Raised Tammie right here. And we played a whole lot a music.

See, we play by ear. We don't play by note. I just play old rough hillbilly. I just play like I play, and that's it.

We always cut ours to suit the people, we just play it like we play at home.

Course, you go down to Nashville why and naturally they're pepped up and hepped up and all the scratch and tuck out and everything. But we just play it like we know it.

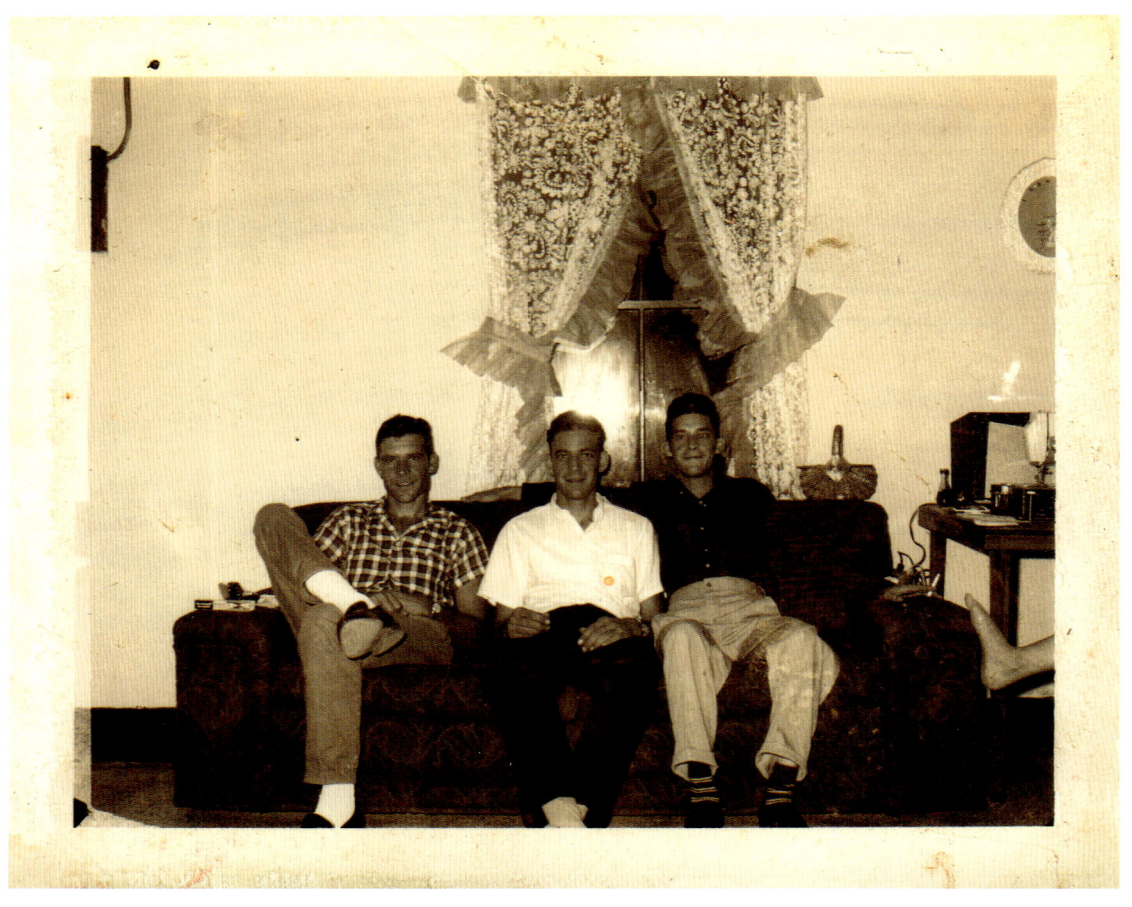

Curtis Byrge (right) and friends, year unknown

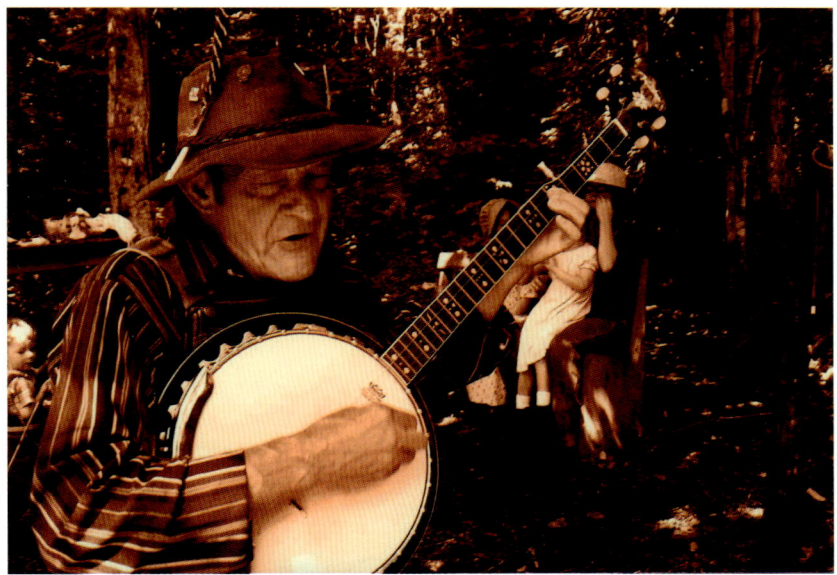

Curtis Byrge, ca. 2010

CURTIS BYRGE

I was born on Christmas Day, 1942, in a coalfield on top of a mountain which we call the Noah Daugherty Mountain. Hard labor over there. And I was born legally blind, so I didn't go to school very much. But my sisters taught me the ABCs. I never could drive anywhere because I couldn't see. So I just walked everywhere. Three or four miles to Elijah's Fork from here. I still walk everywhere today. Every Saturday morning I walk to the flea market to play the fiddle and sing old mountain music. But, you know, being born blind was a good thing, cause God gave me a lot better stuff than I could have learned in school. He gave me the talent to play instruments. At my birth, he bestowed that on me. The Lord did. That's how I become to play and sing. Born knowing.

EUGENE HENSLEY

On 3/3/03, I rededicated my life to Jesus. Got clean camping out in these mountains here. Preached my first sermon in a cave behind a waterfall. Put my Bible down and read the whole Book of John to twelve dogs and a hog. And you know what? Every one of them stayed right there. Did not move or anything, didn't say nothing until I got through and I said "Amen." I looked around at all of them, and they just looked at me, and I said, "Let's go swimming!" Jumped in that pool of water. I never did have a time like that in all my life.

Course, when I first got here, this was my cryin' place, 'cause I was hurt. I would cry until my teardrops was as clear and as fast as this water. And that's what cleaned me out from the inside. This place here with all this water, that's what opened me up and cleaned out all the bitterness. All the hatred. And, man, I tell you what it brings a new creation out of you. The tears is the poison that you keep holdin' back. This was my Valley of Death. I had to die to my old self, another, to receive the new me. The hardest thing that I've had to deal with in my whole life is forgiveness, is to forgive others. And before I could do that I had to learn to forgive me first.

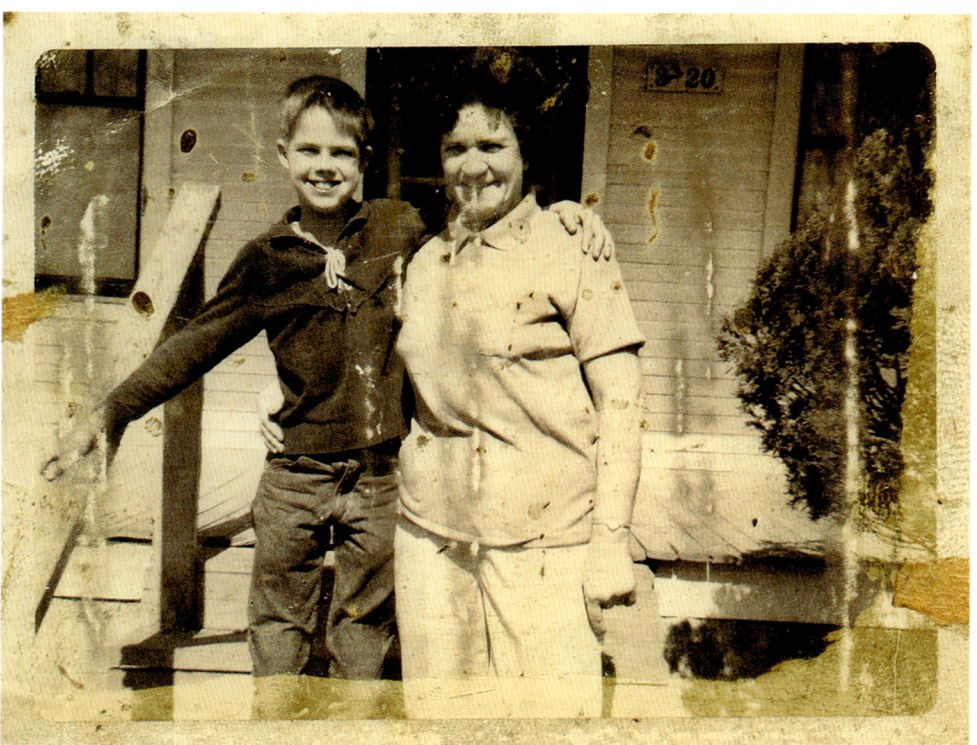

Eugene Hensley with his mother, ca. 1965

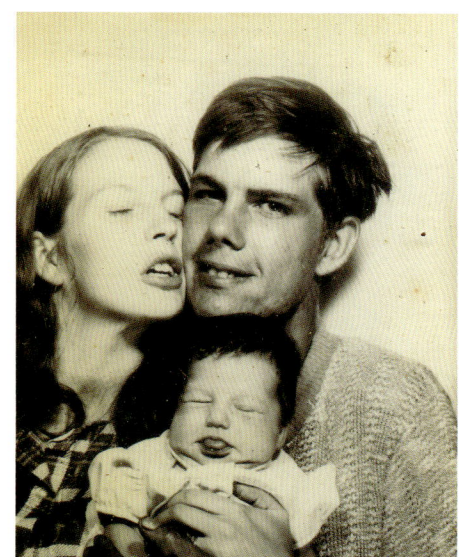

Eugene Hensley
with his wife and
child, ca. 1972

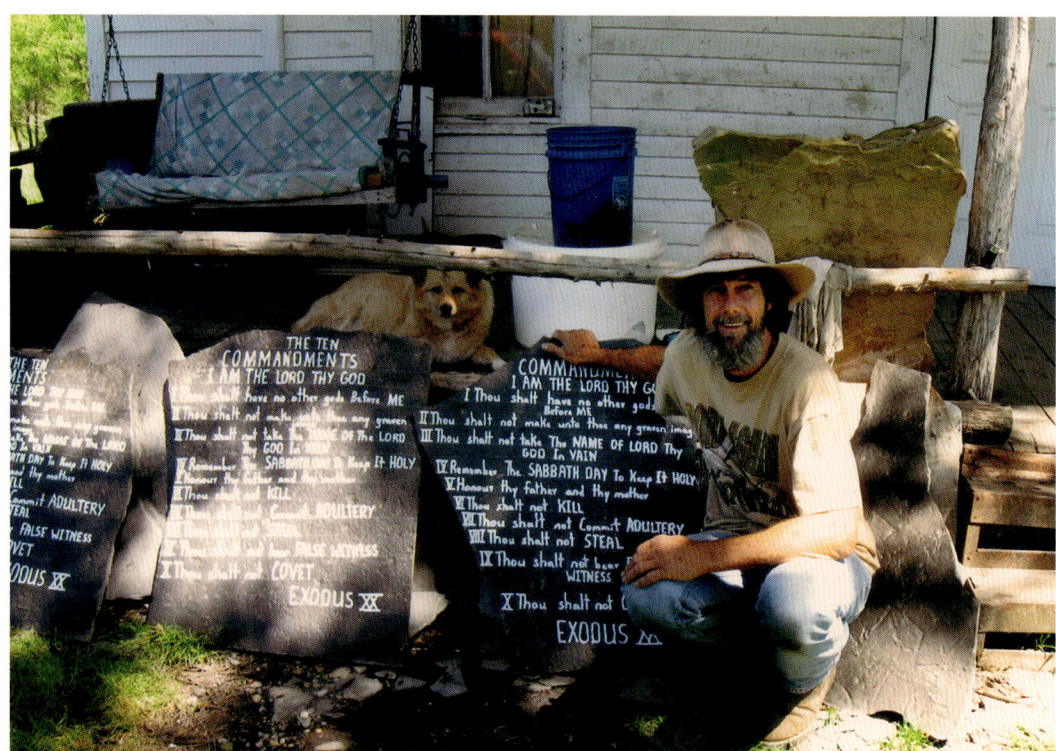

Eugene Hensley in Jamestown, TN, ca. 2010

ACKNOWLEDGMENTS

I must express my great thanks to Sasha Wolf, co-editor of this publication. This work would not have emerged from my own contact sheets had it not been for her honest feedback and incisive understanding.

I am eternally grateful to Bob Fulcher, park ranger, naturalist, folklorist, and musician. Bobby invited me to explore the Cumberland Plateau and was my first guide as I navigated this terrain. Having worked tirelessly for decades as an advocate for both music and the arts, he has a well-earned reputation as someone both personally and professionally interested in preserving the sounds of the region. I am amongst the ranks of many who are currently indebted to Bob for his support of creative traditions in the Cumberland Plateau.

Enormous thanks to Tom Rankin, director of Duke University's MFA|EDA program, for overseeing my post-graduate fellowship that first summer and his continuing mentorship since. It was a great privilege to study with Tom, and my work benefited greatly from his sage advice far after my graduation date.

The Riverview Foundation funded my early work in the region and Bruz Clark always went above and beyond to show special interest in the project.

Thank you to Lisa Volpe for her exquisite essay, which far exceeded my expectations.

Aaron Canipe, Rachel Jessen, and Felicity Palma all provided essential services. Talented artists in their own right, each worked tirelessly to ensure my photographs looked as I intended.

Huge thanks to the team at Daylight Books for believing in the work enough to usher this publication into its finished form.

Many of the oral histories included in *In Their Own Words* were gathered during the process of filming the *Cumberland Folklife* series of documentary films, co-produced by me and Kyle Wilkinson. I must extend my great thanks to Kyle for his hard work and patience. The films are funded by the National Endowment for the Arts and the Tennessee Arts Commission, so further thanks are most certainly warranted there.

Finally, my greatest gratitude belongs with those you have met in these pages, my adopted family in Tennessee. You have welcomed me, you have loved me, and these photographs are a testament to that.

Home on the Range.

I

Oh, give me a home where the buffalo roam, where The dear an the antelope play, where seldom is heard a discouraging word, and the skies are not cloudy all day.

II

Home, home on the range, where The dear & the antelope play, where seldom is heard a discouraging word, and the skies are not cloudy all day.

III

How often at night when The heavens are Bright, with the lights from The glittering star how I stood her amazed and asked as I gazed, if Their glo Exceeds That of ours.

IIII

Oh, give me the sight of the